C000192609

AWAR

BY Angels

THE TRUE STORY OF A VICTIM OF
DOMESTIC VIOLENCE AND HER
JOURNEY OF EMPOWERMENT

Angel Alison Ward

lip

First published in 2012 by:

Live It Publishing
27 Old Gloucester Road
London, United Kingdom.
WC1N 3AX
www.liveitpublishing.com

This is a work of non-fiction. The events and experiences detailed herein
are true and have been faithfully rendered as the author has remembered
them, to the best of her ability. All names and identifying characteristics of
certain individuals have been changed in order to protect their anonymity.

All enquiries should be addressed to Live It Publishing.

ISBN 978-1-906954-44-4 (pbk)

Contents

DEDICATION
Introduction – The Purpose Of This Book

CHAPTER 1
The Day That Changed My Life!
Page 7

CHAPTER 2
The Aftermath
Page 51

CHAPTER 3
Discovering A New Faith
Page 83

CHAPTER 4
New Tools For The Toolbox
Page 117

CHAPTER 5
Inspirations, Coincidences And Teaching The Police
Page 153

CHAPTER 6
Crisis Of Faith
Page 165

Reference

For Gail

A true friend

The Purpose Of This Book

THE PURPOSE of this book is to show you, the reader that from darkness, light will be shown. I experienced a traumatic event that triggered off huge life-changing situations; I had the choice whether to stay a victim or to become empowered. Due to pure grit and determination I was able to discover that deep within me I had the tools I needed that were merely lying dormant. They were to aid my health, well-being and wholeness once more. This book is to give you inspiration, it is to help you recognise guidance and to reassure you that you are not alone. We often have people supporting us in our everyday lives; we must remember that there is a spiritual team of people, guides, angels and even animals who are assisting us also. With practice you can receive their guidance to enable you to live a more fruitful life. Life is not without its difficulties, but by discovering the gifts that you hold within you, by discovering the knowledge, by being still and connecting with your inner core of being, this will allow pure guidance or inspiration to be delivered to you. By denying these tools you deny yourself of many pleasures and much wisdom. Hopefully you will find this book a confirmation that when one uses these tools one truly becomes awakened.

At the end of each chapter, I have acknowledged the lessons learnt and tools discovered. They may be repeated at times throughout the book. You will see through my journey how these tools have grown to become my greatest friends and very welcome gifts.

The Day That Changed My Life!

The pain I felt was more than physical; it was deep, torturing, never-leaving-me pain. I begged God to take my life away – 'give me cancer' I would beg, just anything to end this helpless, painful, ongoing tortuous life! When he didn't answer my pleas I realised I was here to stay... at least for the time being; I couldn't help but feel anger, after all I had been let down by him (God) yet again. How many times can I be left hurt and still be expected to carry on?

You see I always felt that if you lived your life being kind and truthful to people, loving them, helping them, giving passers-by a smile or opening a door, in fact if you took any opportunity to be kind and thoughtful to others, then surely that was our purpose, or so I used to believe. What goes around comes around, right? Well that was how I thought life was meant to be, or at least that was how I lived my life until this torment occurred.

'Get on with it,' I hear you say! 'What happened to cause this pain?' I will tell you, but I ask you to understand that what I am about to share with you is deeply personal and terribly upsetting. I know I must write and publish my story for that is what my guidance has been telling me since the event that I now call The Awakening on Tuesday 5th July, 1994. You see you are going to read about an event that took me to the depths of human sorrow, suffering and humiliation. I have been guided to share this with you in case it wakes you up to your life – maybe you're in an abusive relationship and haven't been able to ask for help yet, or maybe you feel there is more to life but haven't yet found it. I have experienced both; this book tells my story of 'a beautiful gift in an ugly box'. I have been awakened to live my life in trust and LOVE, when once I was a victim in fear and isolation.

I am the child of Paul and Lilian. The first born and only son, Matthew was born in 1961 – the eldest of the brood, he was scary and so much older and more powerful than me. Then there was Nancy, eighteen months older, quite funny but often a bit strange. Then came me, non-descript really; 'pretty but not striking' my mum would say. Last but not least there's Louise, or Boo Boo as we used to call her. The apple of the family's eye and didn't she know it! She could wrap us all round her little finger! Louise is not only my sister, but also a damn good friend as I was to find out. I also have to include the later additions to my family here as they have been so significant in my life: Ken who is Louise's partner, tall dark and handsome; and Elizabeth who is my other sis, married to Matthew – we couldn't have chosen a better sister to join our clan! Our extended family has other additions of nine beautiful children who are a real credit to us all; together we have grown and healed and have created a good solid family base.

But to get back to the love of kindness and truth that I had ingrained in me from a child, there was one occasion where I thought I would experiment with the truth; I felt like being clever so once I actually lied! I was a young girl, maybe about six years old, my dad had summoned us to the kitchen; this meant that someone or something was in trouble. On this occasion, my dad's radio had been broken. The radio was an absolute necessity to my dad as he would listen to his beloved West Bromwich Albion on it if he couldn't get to the away game. He had been a season ticket holder since a boy. Someone had broken his treasured radio and he was determined to find the culprit in his brood of four! As we lined up in the kitchen ready for the interrogation, my knees started to tremble as Dad's voice began to escalate in sound and authority, and he asked us to own up. Of course no one did. I knew I hadn't done it, I would have remembered, right? But the thought of one of us being smacked was too much to bear; those were the days when smacking was acceptable and an integral part of parent/child discipline.

So what did I do? Yes, that's right, I said it was me! God knows why; we had been lined up now for a good while and I was getting more frightened by the long drawn-out process. No one was going to admit it so I decided to be brave or stupid, you decide!

'It was me!' Dad's response was a swift clout and a very long lecture, after which I was banished to bed without tea. Another regular practice in our house if we were naughty.

As I realised in the solitude of my bedroom, it

was not a good plan to lie. I decided there and then that being truthful at all times was to be my new policy. By lying I has misled myself – I thought that by taking responsibility for the deed we would all get back to normal; this was not to be repeated!

So have you got the picture? I am a normal girl, from a normal family, living a normal life. So how could it be that something so abnormal should happen?

Tuesday 5th July, 1994. That was the day that shattered my life and brought me to a depth of despair and pain I never believed possible. I was 29 years old and living as a single mum with my beautiful two and a half year old son, Junior. I was no longer living with Junior's father, Bob. He was physically and mentally abusive to me, and a drinker and regular drug user. We had parted company many times. Initially I returned to try again, believing he would change and I was the person to change him, but then I had become fearful for Junior and I. We finally managed to escape and set up in a little rented house in the West Midlands. I loved our life; we felt safe and the house was cosy, a haven for Junior and I against the world! I had a part time job and Junior attended a state nursery which he loved. I was very proud of the fact I was working. I would have been financially better off on benefits, but I needed to work to retain some self-esteem.

I met Junior's father, Bob in July 1990, when he was working for my dad as a mechanic at the car repair garage. It was obvious there was a physical attraction between us and before we knew it, we were an item. As our relationship began to grow, there were some episodes that caused me concern and made me feel a little uneasy; he would tell me that I was being watched, questioning my every move; often talking about his 'cheating exes'. This alarmed me as there was an underlying threat of violence or oppression. I kept putting it to the back of my mind, as by now I was well and truly in love with this man.

After we had been together for about six weeks, in the mid-summer of 1990, my feeling of unrest and uneasiness grew so much so that I confided my fears to a work colleague and friend and between us my decision was made – I was going to finish with Bob and get back to how I used to be; I hadn't experienced these unpleasant threatening feelings before, it was new territory to me.

So with my mind made up, today was the day that I would call Bob and say it was all over. Then tragedy struck. He called me to tell me his mum had died just a few minutes earlier of a heart attack! He was in a right state, utterly devastated. As I rushed round to his parents' home the realisation hit me that I could not leave him now!

After a few months of tears and 'what ifs', Bob and I had inevitably become close once more; I had pushed my concerns away and had decided that he needed me, so I was to stay. He asked me to move in with him so we became a unit.

It wasn't too long before his previous behaviour returned, this time with a new momentum. It was as if his mum's death had tipped him over the edge; drinking more, disappearing for hours on end and returning in the early hours, is how our life became. I started to lose confidence, and feeling embarrassed and a little ashamed of putting up with his aggressive behaviour I soon became isolated from my friends and family. Looking back it was gradual and subtle to start with, but nevertheless the damage had become evident in my own behaviour; I was now a victim of domestic violence too ashamed to ask for help or leave.

Bob hadn't started the physical abuse as yet, apart from maybe the odd push. It was his mental abuse that really got to the core of me – the constant put me downs, telling me how to dress, calling me too fat, too thin, and ugly! 'All the men laugh when you come into the pub', he would say. 'You know why?' 'No', I would diligently reply. 'Cos you're so ugly!' That was my life and to me there was no way out. It was go further downhill very soon.

I woke up one day and felt unwell; my periods had been heavy and irregular and I had been experiencing cervical pain; so after a trip to the GP, a hospital appointment had followed which led to a date to be operated on for a gynaecological investigation.

The day before I was due to go into hospital, a friend who hadn't seen me for a while popped round uninvited. Jayne expressed concern at my weight loss; I hadn't really noticed but now it had been brought to my attention, I could see that my clothes were hanging off me. After having a lovely chat – so refreshing after the recent verbal lashes from Bob – my friend suggested I took a pregnancy test. We ran to the local chemist to purchase a kit and Jayne waited outside the loo while I tried to pee on the stick...

Yes that's right – I was pregnant! Oh my God, now what was I to do? Many questions rushed through my mind at speed. As Jayne left, congratulating a rather dumbstruck Alison, the reality of this new situation hit me. I was delighted and already in those few minutes loved this baby. Excited and somewhat expectant I rang the father-to-be with the news. Upon his return he announced that he was delighted and that we would become a family. All was well in the world.

No it wasn't, how could I con myself? I had to admit that Bob's behaviour still gave me cause for concern, but he had softened with the news so maybe it would be all right.

My family didn't take the news too well, they offered their congratulations, but we all knew they did not like Bob and thought he wasn't good enough for me. What could I do? I was brought up to believe that you stick together for the sake of the children and part of me wanted it to work. If anyone could change Bob then I could, I would tell myself. I fell totally in love with the baby. I knew I was carrying a boy, call it gut instinct. Getting ready for his arrival was a time of mixed blessings and feelings for me. Bob no longer found me attractive; our physical relationship ended as soon as my tummy grew. Once after barging into the bathroom as I was showering he urged me not to turn around as from behind, I 'still looked like a size 8.' There were also rumours that he was sleeping around with his ex-girlfriend as well as others. Coming home on a Saturday at 4am stinking of booze was the new norm in our household. Again I started to lose myself, to disappear, even with my growing belly.

Just before my due date, 7th December 1991, I started to feel unwell and lost half a stone in a week. I had hardly put any weight on as I was becoming obsessive about returning to my previous size when the baby was born. Maybe then Bob would love me again.

A trip to the doctors meant that my next stay was at the hospital where they could keep an eye on me and the baby. A few days later on the Friday night the rumblings of impending labour began. An uncomfortable night where I endured the pain without asking for help meant that by 6am I was in full labour. The hospital tried calling Bob, but there was no one at home. Eventually he rolled into the labour suite stinking of booze, just in time to see his son born at 11.32am on Saturday 7th December 1991.

He had warned me before the labour that he didn't

want me to be a wimp. He said that I was not to have any painkillers. My stubborn streak reared its head and I obeyed his commands; with a few sneaky puffs of the gas and air before his arrival. Third degree tears meant that I was now in a lot of pain, but still determined to show him I could do it.

Was it worth it? Absolutely! My beautiful, gorgeous and perfect baby boy Junior came into the world and my heart burst open. I had never experienced so much love ever before; and with this new energy came the emergence of a new Alison!

The day we returned home wasn't quite the homecoming I had dreamt of. Slowly walking up the icy path on a cold snowy December afternoon my heart sank as the door opened on a place in disarray. Plates and empty bottles were strewn around the living room. Washing-up was piled high in the kitchen – certainly not the standard of cleanliness you would wish to bring your newborn home.

I decided not to say anything; after all there was much to celebrate. Weary yet happy, I soon settled down to getting the place straight. After getting himself acquainted with his son, Bob then announced that he was off to a Christmas party 'for an hour'. As the front door closed behind him, even after my pleas to stay on our first night home, Bob was off once more into the night... and not just for an hour.

After sobbing and feeling very sorry for myself, I decided to pull myself together. Gathering Junior up I ran his first bath at home. He smelt so lovely and new I couldn't help but take in gulps of his smell, the best perfume ever!

Hours later Junior lay in his cot fast asleep with me in the bed next to him listening out for his cries for feeding or changing. I was brought to an awakened state by hearing the front door lock turn. It was Bob's home time. I decided to pretend I was asleep. This was not the welcome home Bob wanted. As he entered the room he swung the window open stating that fresh air was good for babies. We lived in a mid-terraced house with no central heating or double glazing. Although Junior was swaddled, his resulting cries were of a volume that Bob had not experienced previously. Not happy, and shoving me harshly, Bob instructed me to keep him quiet.

A long, fitful night followed. Eventually when Bob had fallen into his drunken slumber I quietly slipped from the bed and closed the window.

A few more weeks followed of Bob displaying

increasingly unreasonable and unbalanced behaviour; I was not coping well. Junior was not sleeping through yet, and without the support of my partner I started to feel even more isolated. I decided that I just couldn't do it anymore. It all came to a head when he returned late again hours after the pub had shut, reeking of booze and acting very unpredictably. Normally I could respond in a way that would pacify him, however I started to feel very alarmed and I knew that our lives were in danger. Again I was in bed pretending to be asleep as Bob entered the room. I was picking up that he thought it was time to play, and not the enjoyable sort of playing. 'Get up, I want to talk to you' he said. He then ranted on in a language I did not understand. Then to my horror he scooped Junior up out of his cot, flung open the window and started to dangle him out of the window. Horror and absolute fear gripped me! Knowing that I had to use all my powers of persuasion I eventually convinced him to return Junior to me, his mum. With the baby in my arms the opportunity to escape was now in sight. Taking full advantage of Bob's drunken state, I ran down the stairs, grabbing the nappy bag as I left the house, car keys in hand. Throwing Junior in the car seat and securing him as best I could with my trembling hands I drove off into the night towards home.

Minutes later my parents opened the door; had they been expecting me? Mum took Junior with only the gentleness that a mother and Nan could do as Dad, ever practical, poured me a brandy.

It was decided that I would live with my parents until I sorted myself out. Whatever that meant! To my amazement, something rose up within me and challenged this idea. Maybe despite what had happened I still needed to make my relationship work with Junior's dad. Maybe it was me who was at fault – Bob would often tell me that I was ugly, repulsive and totally hopeless as both a mother and a homemaker. 'Maybe you are at fault' I told myself. My self-esteem had taken such a battering that not only was I taking the blame, but somehow my thoughts were telling me to accept the way he treated me; it was what I deserved.

Each day I sunk even lower into the pit of shame of being me. My only ray of hope was Junior. A bonny lad, he brought me so much joy. I couldn't love anyone as much as I loved Junior.

As I returned to Bob's home my parents and Louise were unable to hide their dismay. Not able to hold in her thoughts, Louise exclaimed 'Can't you see what he's doing to you?' The answer to that although not spoken aloud was 'no'. I couldn't see anymore; I was sinking and slipping away. You could see the weight slipping off me as if to confirm it. I was disappearing in front of my family's eyes and I was unable to do anything about it. How despondent they must have been! I'm so sorry that they had to endure that.

I have spoken with many women who have experienced domestic violence and abusive relationships since that time in my life. They all spoke of losing themselves and not seeing or believing there were any choices open to them. It's as if the abuser takes their power away continually; this cycle ever increases and the "victim" is left feeling they have no power to make decisions. Trapped in the ever growing cycle of despair!

I have managed to block out most of the physical abuse including spitting in my face and pushing and slapping, yet the most painful of all was the mental torture. A daily dose was prescribed by this man and I duly accepted it; that was all I was worth wasn't it?

Although I was now a fully fledged victim, my awareness grew that Bob and I were never going to work; this may be obvious to you as the reader, but with me it took a while longer. I hated the thought of being a single parent and the judgement that goes with it. He was sleeping around and up to his old tricks. Painfully aware that I was not after all the person to change this man, I came to accept that I couldn't stay stay with him and I was also probably going to be on my own for the rest of my life. Who would want this excuse of a woman, I would ask.

Moving on

Finally I left Bob for the last time and my parents welcomed me back yet again whilst I searched for a new home. Junior loved this time at his Nan and Grandad's. He would go out with Grandad on a Saturday to do 'men's jobs'; going to the butchers for the Sunday roast and sausages for lunch, or dogs c***s as my dad would call them. Remember he was a mechanic by trade; this was his language. Not offensive coming from Dad.

Eventually as I started to blossom in the bosom of my family, a small two-bed modern terraced house became available just a twenty minute walk away and just down the road from the office where I worked.

Each morning I would walk down the road with Junior in his pushchair, get the bus to nursery, then do the return journey to work. When the working day ended I would once more board the bus to collect Junior, then make the return journey. For Junior and me these were special times. We would sing songs, march like soldiers, then go and play in the park before returning for tea. My friends would often join us, creating much laughter and joy for all concerned. I loved looking after Junior; bathing him and cooking fresh food on a very limited budget – thank God for garlic and herbs! Mum always said Junior smelt of garlic whenever she saw him... or smelt him!

We were blessed to have lovely neighbours, Jason and Nigel, a couple who made us very welcome. Nigel was a chef in an old people's home. He loved Junior and would often bring some 'spare food' home. I think he knew money was tight as I was still quite thin. I often went to bed hungry, but as long as Junior was fed, I was happy. I was a proud girl and hadn't learnt the art of asking for help at this time.

As Bob was Junior's father, he still played a part in Junior's life, although somewhat irregular. He would often pop round uninvited, occasionally give some money towards his upkeep and be a dad when it suited him. Sometimes I would wish that we were all still a family irrespective of what went on before. There were times when we acted like we were, but it always ended in tears with Bob storming off because I was at home with Junior and unable to go out to have fun in the evenings. I think he actually enjoyed the power of that.

Once, Bob invited Junior and I to spend some time with him at his brother's house in North Devon. He suggested that if it went well we might consider getting back together. You know, I actually contemplated that. I must point out that my gut feeling said no, it doesn't feel right, but again I wanted to be a family and thought that maybe there was a glimmer of hope for us.

The whole trip was a blessing in disguise; I saw Bob with fresh eyes with his verbal put-downs, constantly belittling me, telling his brother and his partner what a bad mum I was.... But the breaking point was when Bob started to smoke cannabis in front of Junior. I have always been strongly against drug-taking especially when little ones are around. That was a huge no for me and any feelings that I still had for Bob dissipated with the smoke from his cigarette.

The return journey home was frightening. Never being a good driver Bob kept swerving all over the motorway. Praying until we got home, Junior and I arrived exhausted. Upon opening my front door, a sudden wave of strength poured into me; I announced that there was and would never be a future for Bob and me after the weekend and that he was no longer welcome in my home. Alternative arrangements would need to be made for visiting Junior.

Closing the door on Bob that night was the beginning of a new life for Junior and me. I had found a strength in me that had lain dormant for too long. No way was I going to be pushed around or bullied any more.

I started to feel good. Yes, good about myself. What a welcome feeling this was. I thought it had gone forever. I started to get the old me back. Family and friends commented that I looked better than I had in an age. Bob's input into Junior's life was still irregular, occasionally picking him up or having him for the odd overnight stay. I had tried to set up something more structured, but that wasn't Bob's way. What was I to do? He was still his dad and Junior loved him. Surely I had to allow him to see

Junior, although I was never comfortable with Bob being alone with Junior; he didn't look after him as I did and that caused me concern. Life was full of couples who had parted, of that I was aware, and if they managed it then surely I had to make it work for Junior's sake.

After one of Bob's impromptu visits I communicated in no uncertain terms, that this was not good enough; Junior deserved better that this. I told him that if he was unable to adhere to regular pre-arranged visits then he wouldn't see him at all. Junior had started to play up when Bob let him down by not collecting him when promised. This was too much to bear, Junior had been through enough! Bob left stating that he would 'pull his socks up'.

It was about this time, in May 1994, that a friend whom I had met through Bob told me that I needed to get out more. Jackie was also a work colleague now and we had grown quite close. I suppose I had become a bit of a recluse, yet I was happy with the life Junior and I had created.

The spring days started to show real promise as the sun shone and the temperature began to rise; it was the sort of weather that urged you to be outside. Jackie tried to encourage me, as did Gail and Jessie, my other close school friends, and of course my sister Louise. 'It won't hurt you to go out' they would say. 'We'll look after Junior.' But I just didn't want to leave him. It was then that Jackie came up with a suggestion that I couldn't resist.

'We're all going to this lovely pub on Sunday', she said. 'Everyone's going to be there on their motorbikes, it's near a canal where the barges float past, plus the play area will encourage Junior to join in with the other children. He'll still have you close by.' How could I refuse, it sounded like too good an opportunity to miss.

'Ok!' I said. 'I'll come, but I haven't got any spare cash!' Jackie offered to pay, but unable to accept this help I sneaked £5 out of the housekeeping.

The sun shone and my hands trembled at the thought of being out with a group of people. Socialising had become so alien to me, my nerves definitely started to take hold. Junior soon snapped me out of it as his excitement at seeing the boats and playing on the swings took over.

As we approached the large crowd of people my shyness increased – sitting down in an area where I could be relatively unnoticed but still see Junior my attention was drawn to a quiet man. His name was

Carl, a name I had never liked! I used to joke with friends I could never go out with a Carl let alone marry one. I was soon to be proved wrong.

Carl told me that he was separated from his wife and that in six week's time he was due to go on a ten-week bike tour of Europe with his friend. When I heard this, I found myself thinking 'well there's no way we're getting involved then if he's off in a few weeks.' This somewhat surprised me as I had absolutely no desire to be in a relationship with anyone!

Whether we were in denial that day or not; something happened to us both. We found each other; we didn't express it in words; we knew.

Returning home I sensed a feeling of lightness return; was this a glimpse of happiness? Although this feeling of lightness and happiness grew, it confused me. Why would I have feelings, or the emergence of feelings, for a stranger? A stranger who was due to go away in six week's time? There was a sense of inevitability looming. Hesitancy yet excitement started to grip me.

The following Friday I was coerced into going out again; twice in one week, whatever next? This time Junior was staying at home tucked up in bed;

miraculously Louise, now six months pregnant with her first child, appeared informing me that she was babysitting for the night while I was to go out. Jackie and Louise were obviously up to matchmaking.

The same group of bikers and friends had a regular meeting each Friday at a pub in Warwickshire. Loads of banter, as well of course discussions of bikes, bike parts, servicing, bike routes.

This Friday was the first night I had been out on my own for what seemed a lifetime, but I was Jackie's guest and she promised she would look after me. As Jackie's husband drove there on his bike, she picked me up in the car and I shared my nerves and fears at the recent meeting of souls. Of course I wasn't told Carl was going to be there, but as soon as I walked in, I felt his presence. Blushing, yet a little excited I smiled and thought how sweet it was that people cared for me in this way. Although some of the group were a bit scary to me in appearance, they welcomed me with open arms. The women were lovely too, so welcoming. They all knew about Bob and how badly I had been treated.

Carl and I found ourselves sitting next to each other and we started to hold hands under the table without even speaking. A surreal experience soon became very relaxed, much chatting and laughter followed. There was clearly some magic going on that night. It was as if a greater force was placing us together that night; I must say I was relaxed and enjoying myself yet again. I thought I could get used to this more relaxed state!

Carl and I continued to meet up regularly; I even invited him to my house. Junior was in bed as I didn't want to introduce them formally as it was far too soon. Besides Junior came first and I didn't want him getting confused. He had been through enough in his two and a half years.

We became very close very quickly, and although we both recognised and acknowledged this we were also aware that Carl's trip was drawing closer. So we decided that if we still felt the same way on his return we would continue our growing friendship.

Carl's departure date was 4th July 1994 – we met and said our goodbyes. I had bought him a St. Christopher pendant to keep him safe on his journey; this touched Carl as he knew I didn't have spare cash for gifts. As he accepted it his smile filled my heart, I knew there was love for him.

As we said goodbye, there was a part of me that was very relieved that we were to be away from each other for a while. I told myself I would use this time to sort my head out and decide if this was what I wanted. I already knew the answer but I was trying to fight it; you see I enjoyed being this new independent woman without a man telling me what to do, how to act, what to wear. Saying that, I knew Carl was not the sort of man who treated women in such a way. The air of inevitability was still present and increasing. Where will it all end I asked myself?

Although this new part of my life brought me excitement, happiness and a certain freedom, I hadn't yet informed my family and friends about the telephone calls I'd been receiving. The phone would ring all through the night, and upon answering a man's disguised voice would tell me to 'watch my back' or 'you're going to die'. This, coupled with Junior starting to be agitated at night and woken by nightmares, started to trouble me. This was a burden I didn't wish to share. Could this be Bob? The voice didn't sound like his, but who else would know my number and say such things? I decided to ask the police for help only to be told that without witnesses there was nothing I could do; I had no proof. Previous to this I was awoken one night by a nightmare in which Bob was trying to kill Junior and me. I dismissed this as being overly sensitive, a trait which I often adopted. 'Pull yourself together girl,' I told myself. But just to make sure there was nothing I could do, I rang a local solicitor to ask advice. 'I'm sure it's my ex... he said he's going to kill me.' Again, without proof what was I to do?

So there we were: sitting ducks waiting for the inevitable to happen, or was I just being silly?

On the evening of Carl's departure, (Independence Day in the States, how apt!) Gail my school friend of seventeen years came round to catch up on all my news. I wasn't really in the mood to chat, Louise had even suggested earlier that I stay at Mum's as they had got wind of the phone calls and were worried. Gail insisted she was coming round – 'it's better than watching Coronation Street, listening to you and your life' she announced. How could I resist her company?

I told her all about Carl and my new group of friends, told her how the whole experience was surreal. Gail, being the open-minded and spiritual person she was, loved hearing all this. As we shared a pack of cigarettes, a treat we would share on our get-togethers, I proceeded to share my news and the recent threats and phone calls. Gail was understandably concerned and begged me to stay at my parents'. As we talked pieces of the jigsaw started to come together; Dad had asked me earlier in the week why Bob's van had been parked outside my house late at night on consecutive nights. Dad had adopted a habit of driving past to see if all was well in the previous few weeks, probably under instruction from Mum.

I knew that Bob was behind the calls, but if I recognised and accepted it was him then that meant we really were in danger. Right?

As all the pieces started to slot into place, I realised that Bob had parked his van outside, maybe giving the appearance of happy families. He was there so he could watch what I was up to, keeping an eye on me. The dream I had a few days earlier had really been to warn me. I recalled that my grandad was in the dream and Junior was named after my favourite grandparent, a great man who made a real impact on me.

It was all becoming incredibly clear. Our lives were in danger and it was imminent. Gail tried all she could to calm me down, but there was no getting away from it, in my mind it was now fact!

To detract from the growing sense of drama, Gail

produced her favourite tarot cards from her bag. We would often give each other readings and actually we were getting very good, Gail in particular. Slowly she shuffled the cards then handed them over to me. I in turn then shuffled them and chose seven cards. Gail's face showed a look of horror as the cards delivered their meanings. All the sword cards were looking at us. The card that stood out was The Smiler with the Knife.

'Watch your back, there is someone in your life who feigns friendship, but who really wants to hurt you' was the card's explanation.

As Gail threw the cards down she begged me to be careful. 'Please go to your mum's' she begged. I tried to calm us both down and became practical. 'We're over-reacting, let's just calm down. What on earth do you think will happen to us?' As we started to calm down, I found myself ceremoniously, yet somewhat unconsciously, tearing the pages of my diary out up until the 4th July. 'Why have you done that?' Gail asked. 'I don't know, I just know something big is going to happen. Something really big.' Then I slumped down into the chair and became oddly calm.

We didn't have to wait too long to find out.

The day of the awakening

The dawn of a new day brought hope along with the sunshine. Upon awakening I felt warmed by the sun flooding through the window, but there was a feeling of trepidation and anxiety that took away the feeling of lightness. The night's previous events came flooding back and then I recalled that Bob wasn't going to be in the area for a few weeks. He had got a cash in hand job in Devon and would be staying with his brother. What a relief; a few days off from the persistent phone threats, at last a sense of relief. As I tended to Junior the anxiety came back and wouldn't leave me; it grabbed my gut and started to twist it around, coupled with a sense of nausea. No matter what I told myself, my body was telling me something totally different.

As I left Junior at his nursery, I made a point of telling the staff to keep an extra vigilant eye on Junior today and under no circumstances was anyone else to collect him unless I gave written or verbal instruction. What brought this on? Well the previous week, as I returned to collect Junior, Bob was there also 'collecting' Junior although it hadn't been previously agreed. He was surprised to see me as I was a good fifteen minutes early. I recalled that this made me suspicious and uneasy at the time. Was I over reacting though? Bob is his father, he has rights too. As I once more pushed the alarm bells to the side, I had written a letter to the head of the nursery explaining that only I had full parental responsibility as Bob and I had never married and that he was not to take Junior without my consent. Bob didn't appreciate being told, and after hurling some foul language at me he drove off in his white van!

So getting back to the sunny day of Tuesday 5th July 1994, as usual, after dropping Junior off I made the return journey to my part time job at the office – a job I enjoyed on the whole particularly since Jackie worked there too. We often had a laugh when the boss was out and there were no customers in, which was a regular occurrence.

My thoughts then went to Carl and I wondered where he was right now. Dismissing the feeling almost immediately, I told myself I did not have time for this.

After an uneventful day and feeling very tired, Junior and I returned straight home. No park visit today, all the previous broken nights' sleep due to the phone calls had caught up with me. When we arrived home, we had a pleasant surprise. Louise, now just over eight months pregnant, had decided to pay us a visit. Looking tired but happy at the prospect at being a mum, Louise explained that the visit was to try and convince me to go and stay at my parents' for a few days as everyone was worried about us. 'I can't Lou, I just have to get on with life, I can't be gripped by fear every time the phone rings.' But I was.

As I gently pushed Louise out of the front door, I found myself promising I would call Mum and arrange to stay for a few days in a few days' time. Satisfied and suddenly feeling very pregnant, Louise knew she was beaten and returned home to await the arrival of her little one.

I told Junior that I was going to start cooking tea while he watched his TV programme and that if he needed me he knew where I was. The home was so tiny it would have been very difficult to lose anyone: a small hallway with a tiny kitchen leading off, and a lounge straight in front was the downstairs; the upstairs consisted of Junior's bedroom at the front, a little bathroom in the middle and my bedroom at the back overlooking a small but amply proportioned garden.

Spag bol was on the menu tonight. If I made a large pan I could add some extra tomatoes and it would last for two, possibly three meals. Junior loved sucking up the 'worms' as we called them. He loved being covered in the red sauce all over his face and lips even more. No worries though, the bath would soon have him back to a gleaming child with angelic features!

A knock at the door made me jump. I must stop being so nervous I told myself. 'Scared of your own shadow' my grandad would say, how right was he now?

Imagine my surprise when opening the door Bob was standing there. 'What are you doing here? I thought you were in Devon?'

'I was but I'm here now' he said. 'I think we need to discuss Junior and my access.'

At long last he had realised that to be a good dad to Junior he needed to provide stability, security and routine. Maybe all my nagging had paid off. I scanned him over all too briefly and invited him in, quickly turning the gas off under the spaghetti sauce as we passed the kitchen.

He looked clean, his hair was washed, not greasy as it had been the last time I saw him, maybe just maybe he's becoming more reasonable I concluded.

Imagine my surprise then when walking into the lounge, Bob ignored Junior. How long had it been since he last saw Junior? I couldn't remember. Why is he ignoring him I questioned silently? As I tried to make sense of what was going on, I caught a whiff of alcohol. The realisation hit me that – shit, I shouldn't have let him in. I certainly wouldn't have had I smelt it upon opening the door. Remembering how violent he gets under the influence of alcohol, my anxiety returned.

Feeling vulnerable and at the same time trying to work out if I needed to come up with an escape plan, I was interrupted by a sharp flash of pain. Bang! My face! Bang again! My face! No surely this is not happening... Bob had headbutted me twice in quick succession and was now telling me 'I don't want you but I don't want anyone else to have you.'

My mind started to race, is this really happening? Junior looked bewildered and frightened. My little boy, my gorgeous little boy, I couldn't stand the thought of him witnessing this. Again my thoughts were interrupted, this time by Bob speaking. 'I've planned it all, I'm going to kill you. Today is the day you're going to die and no one can help you. I know all about you and Carl, I watched him go. Today is the day that you are going to die and you will be all alone, no one will find you. Then I'm going to kill me and Junior.'

'No please' I shrieked, 'God no, not Junior. I'll do anything please Bob please, please!'

By now blood was pouring from my lips; the top one had split in two. Bob proceeded to tell me about his plan, he informed me that no one knew he was here, and he had alibis who would state that he was with them, his brother in Devon being one of them.

The torture had well and truly begun.

I had to think and quickly. Out of the corner of my eye I could see Junior starting to react; a panic set in. Then a glint of a knife interrupted my thoughts. Bob had produced a knife from his back pocket. 'He means this, he really means this' I told myself. My dream was true, Gail's cards were true, and my gut instincts were true. Today is really the day I'm going to die. Twenty nine years old! So many thoughts, so many fears tumbled down all at once. As I was trying to work out what to do, another headbutt came down. This time in full force, he then repeatedly banged my head against the wall. By now Bob had manoeuvred me into the corner and was straddled across me; I was trapped, with no escape. My head started to swim and consciousness slipped away, I could see the knife; it was now in front of my face. This was the knife that had been missing from my kitchen drawer; how long had he planned this?

The next stage was inevitable; he started to stab at my chest. The piercing pain gripped me as the blood shot across the room in short sharp bursts. So many things happening all at once, was I watching a horror movie? I wasn't sure. The reality hit me; it was a horror movie and we were the cast.

I knew I had to somehow remain conscious. If I gave into the fear and pain, we would surely die; it would be too easy to kill me and Junior, my baby, my God my baby! I'm his mum, it's my job to protect him. Naturally yet quite bizarrely, I started to sing nursery rhymes in my head 'Hickory, dickory dock, the mouse ran up the clock...' trying to focus on each word, then yet another blow reminded me I was being killed, murdered in front of my little boy, two and a half years old.

Junior decided he had to help, he jumped on Bob's back telling him to stop, "Daddy no!" my brave boy kicked and punched his father with all his might. Begging Junior to move away so he wouldn't fall victim to the knife, he did as I told him to do.

Junior continued to try so many other things all to no avail. He placed my glasses next to me that I used to watch TV, that didn't work so he fetched his precious dressing gown belt that he used to suck and place in the corner of his eye when he felt sleepy. Bob paid no attention to him, he just kept on going. Junior then let out a howling animal-like noise, then fled to his potty where he sat; again trying to deflect Bob's attention. I could see all this even in the midst of this horrific ordeal. By this time I had brought my leg up to protect my heart and chest and I felt the knife penetrate deep into my shin area, I knew my time was coming to an end and I felt myself succumb to the blood seeping and shooting from my body and I became very woozy.

This wooziness led to me somehow leaving my body; yes, I left my shell of a bloody body in my living room with Junior and that monster and I found myself moving at speed, being taken down a light-filled tunnel in a roller coaster motion. Snapshot photos appeared on either side of me, all people whom I had met over the years, some forgotten by the passage of time. This journey was moving ever faster, my short hair being blown back against my head. Trying to make sense of what was happening was not possible; a part of me accepted it, the inevitability of death and dying. I couldn't go back to Junior now, yet somehow I knew he would be ok. Don't ask me how I knew, I just did. It's incredible to think that the human mind responds on so many levels, in so many ways during trauma and situations such as this.

So the journey of light continued, I was now in flow, no more fighting, thinking or resisting.

Just ahead of me, a huge ball of light started to draw near or was I drawing close to it? I wasn't sure; the light was so bright, so radiant yet it didn't hurt my eyes. This ball of light brought with it an overwhelming feeling of comfort, love and no pain. Inviting me closer I started to experience pure joy and then I saw him. My lovely grandad who Junior was named after was standing at the point of a triangle of people. Yes it was definitely him; looking younger, fitter, even more handsome (if that was possible). Was this my welcoming committee? I knew all these other people yet I didn't recognise them. The love pouring towards me was so overwhelming; words cannot describe the emotion and limitlessness of their love. Yes I wanted to go to him and hug him, tell him how much I love him and have missed him.

If this was dying, I'm up for it, I told myself as I drew ever closer.

Then a new reality hit me, Junior needed me, I was twenty-nine years old, too young to die and I had to save Junior. You may be thinking that my reactions to openly leaving this life and Junior sound bizarre or even callous; I have to admit they do to me as I'm writing this. All I can say is, this is the truth of how I remember it, as odd as it may sound. We were in a very unusual, surreal situation where 'normal' thoughts do not make sense.

From the depths of these realisations I heard a voice talk to me. An old fashioned Brummy voice (a Birmingham accent, for those of you who don't know the colloquialism).

'It's not time to go yet duck,' she said, whoever she was. Suddenly I was back in my living room; Grandad had disappeared; so had the tunnel. I was facing Bob. Blood covered the wall and the carpet. Looking down at myself, it was evident that my physical body was in a mess. Then, out of nowhere or even somewhere, calmness swept over me; 'What would your mum, your beloved mum who died three years ago, say if she saw you doing this to me and Junior?'

As the question registered with my attacker, two things happened at precisely the same time; firstly Bob pulled back, and let out a holler of a moan, pulling back the knife – I knew this was my time to die. No fear came from me this time, I was ready for the final raining of hatred this man had for me. He could no longer hurt me whatever the outcome now; I had discovered a kind of faith. As the preparation for the final lunge loomed, the doorbell rang and Nigel's voice shouted 'Bob leave her alone, I've called the police and they're on their way.' Interrupting his motion, Bob pulled further back, giving me an escape route. I took it. Managing to scramble my small six stone frame out of this newly formed gap, I lurched forwards and ran to the front door. Flight or fight was the new choice and I was taking advantage of it. He got up and pulled my hair as my fingers scrambled at the lock. The door flung open, and out I ran as Nigel stood there in horror at what was before him. 'Bob leave her, put the knife down, you've done enough damage.' Bob was having none of it, as I ran a few yards to the local corner shop yelling my instructions to get the police, he grabbed Junior and ran out of the house flashing the blood stained knife at Nigel.

Nigel my lovely, kind next door neighbour was the saviour of the day. He was to tell me later that he was at work, cooking the patients' evening meal at the old people's home when something told him to go home. Thank God he listened to his intuition, guidance, call it what you will. On returning home he heard the noise and screams coming from our house and called the police. He then had the guts to ring the doorbell and attempt to talk Bob out of the attack. What an absolutely brave man.

I was now being forced into a chair at the corner shop. Owned by a lovely Sikh family, Junior and I would visit there each day. They often gave Junior a lolly, a treat for his good manners.

Shocked by my appearance they attempted to calm me down and dress my wounds. I brushed them off. 'Junior, he's got my Junior, you must help me.' By now the police had arrived and were gently placing me into the back of a police car where they inspected the wounds.

Mum was telephoned, I somehow in my shock shouted out her number and someone made that call my mum was dreading yet expecting. She ran all the way and arrived just as I was being placed in the ambulance. Shocked with the full reality my mum pulled herself back from falling. She was amazing, burying her hurt, after all this was her wounded baby in front of her and where was Junior? I spurted everything out in an instant; the whole lot. Then I begged Mum to get Junior. It was then that we were told that Bob had taken Junior in an unknown car and was last seen speeding off in the opposite direction on the wrong side of the road. The police had announced it across the radio waves, even the local radio station announced it to warn other drivers. It was now approaching 6pm, rush hour, home time for many.

The next stage was the worst I have ever experienced in the whole of my life, the realisation that Junior could be dead. I cannot explain how it felt and I feel immense sorrow for those who have lost a child. I started to tell myself I needed to prepare for the worst.

The ambulance crew took over and I let them eventually, after saying I couldn't go until I heard about Junior. My energy depleted and feeling hopeless, my physical body started to give in to the shock. Lifting me into the ambulance, a kind officer calmly and gently informed me that Junior had been found... alive! He was on his way to the local hospital and was safe. My body then slumped and succumbed to the weight of the shock. The full force of what had happened started to hit me.

LESSONS LEARNT

- *Listen to your guidance, your body will respond as it tries to get the 'Danger' message across.*

- *Ask for help; sharing the weight of a burden or problem with a trusted love one lifts the weight; more shared solutions appear.*

- *Forgive yourself! A biggy!*

- *Keep a dream diary by your bed to record your dreams and any thoughts that are restricting sleep.*

- *If it doesn't feel right, don't do it; if it does, go for it!*

"Angel" Alison Ward

The Aftermath

We were told that it was a miracle that Junior had been found. Miracle! That word kept popping up; it was a miracle that Nigel came home because he listened to his intuition, guidance, call it what you will; a miracle nonetheless. Now we were been told finding Junior was a miracle too, what was going on? Was there a greater force acting to protect us after all?

When the police made the call over the radio to their officers, a newly qualified, young PC didn't respond straight away, she sat still and asked herself 'what would I do if I thought I've killed my ex, then want to go somewhere to end my life and my son's?' Knowing the area well, she found herself driving to a well-known little pocket of countryside in an industrial part of the Midlands. A passer-by alerted her and her colleague to a man acting suspiciously near some bushes. He was in fact pulling some bushes over his car while the engine was running, with a man-made tube attached to the exhaust.

Calling for back-up, they slowly approached the vehicle; they saw Junior being held firmly on Bob's lap as carbon monoxide poured into the car... and Junior's lungs. When Junior's back arched they knew they had to act swiftly, instructing Bob to free Junior and open the door, but this was not an option Bob had considered. Knowing Junior's life was in danger – how much carbon monoxide can a small body take? – they broke the side window and pulled Junior out in an instant while also arresting Bob. Thank God the ordeal was over!

But it was only just beginning.

Hours passed and the staff at A&E were so loving and careful with me; knowing the trauma I'd been through they treated me with such care and attention. Lying flat out on a surgical bed in just my pants, they assessed the damage. I thought to myself, if the miracles hadn't occurred this could have been a mortuary slab rather than a bed in A&E.

Wounds to my chest: one two and a half inches deep, and they measured it by placing a special ruler inside the wound. Neck and slash wounds to my face: the deeper one where Bob held the knife against my neck informing me of his plans. Split lip, deep wound to my left leg, slashed nipple, bruised ribs, considerable bruising around my body, plus a splitting headache were the results of the thirty minute attack. It was noticed that my hearing was affected too; that will be the shock I was told. It will soon return.

It didn't.

Another miracle was placed into the 'Miraclepot' – if my breasts had been larger the knife would have been able to penetrate deeper, therefore puncturing a lung or the heart. Thank God then for small boobs, never again would I complain about my 'fried eggs' as Louise would call them, or 'hiccups' as I liked to add.

The newspaper reported the story as 'local interest' the next day; superficial wounds is what they said I had – 'SUPERFICIAL WOUNDS!'

I was told Junior was doing well, he had settled down for the night and was relatively unscathed from the day's dramas.

Refusing to stay in hospital overnight for an assessment of my head injury, I discharged myself. How could I stay there? I was convinced Bob would have sent someone to 'finish the job'. He wanted me dead; nothing was going to stop him. I needed to be with Mum and Dad, to be their little girl again. To be held and told everything would be all right. Junior and I needed to be reunited without delay!

The local hospital's secure unit meant that I couldn't visit Junior. I had to go home to my parents, leaving my little house, our home all in darkness, and Junior without his mum.

Bob meanwhile was locked in a police cell, joking with his captors. Two counts of attempted murder, my blood on his shirt, he was soon to be taken to the Magistrates Court.

The shock of my dad's face is something I never want to see again. My dad – a man's man, big and tough with dry, hard hands from years of manual work – shock was alien to him. Until now.

Mobile phones weren't commonplace in 1994, so when Mum tried to contact Dad by telephone at work she was unsuccessful. Leaving a scrawled message near the phone as she rushed out to my aid, Dad returned home a little while later. The house being silent was not what he was used to, with no sign of Lil his wife. Wondering why it was so quiet, Dad was disturbed by the telephone ringing. It was the police telling him that his daughter had been attacked and was in hospital, he was to come at once.

Still in his work clothes, covered in oil, Dad drove on autopilot to be greeted by the state of his daughter and the unfolding story.

I couldn't put my clothes on as they were either covered in blood, or had been cut from my body, so Dad collected a spare work top from his car. I felt quite indignant that my clothes has been damaged and taken away. Strange I thought to think that way.

Once back at my parents, Dad insisted on giving me a brandy to 'calm my nerves'. It stung so sharply through my sutured lips. But not to be outdone, my dad got me a straw. Not any old straw; a blue one, my favourite!

As I poured out the day's events and Dad poured another brandy, we all suddenly realised that it might be on the local radio news. It was. Too late, our family and friends would hear about it in this way. Mum called Louise, insisting all was well so as not to alarm her heavily pregnant daughter. Louise was having none of this pacification. Minutes later, she arrived on the doorstep considerably distressed. Ken followed behind her.

'What has that bastard done to you?'; she didn't need to ask any more questions as my battered and bruised face answered some of them.

I felt Louise's pain; this was not what I wanted, the ripple effect was beginning to surface.

The following day the trauma continued.

After a night where sleep evaded me, the new day didn't bring hope. Weary and bruised to the bone, I lifted my tired body out of bed. I was walking with a stick as the wound to my leg made it difficult to walk. Every part of me ached; even my hair carried the wounds inflicted just over twelve hours earlier. The reality of this new morning reminded me how quiet the house was without Junior there, certainly not what I was used to.

The first task was to get some information on how Junior was doing; they didn't tell me much. Were they withholding information on my son? What right had they got?

I wasn't giving up that easy; after several phone calls from me, Mum and Louise, we were told to go to the hospital later on that day; about 5pm. But before this I had the police interrogation to come.

Firstly I was instructed to go along to the local Police Station so I could give a blood sample to prove that the blood that Bob was wearing was in fact my blood. Did they not believe me? Were the injuries not enough? All these questions and doubts added to the dull, aching depression engulfing me. Dad drove me there and waited in the waiting room as I diligently did as I was told. Unbeknown to me, Bob was still in the holding cell. He got wind that I was there and was able to shout out at me. He continued to torture me whilst I gave my blood.

Upon my return, it was time to collect Junior. The sky turned grey with our mood and the rain came pelting down. Dad drove us towards the hospital and we became stuck in the rush hour traffic. Twenty-four hours previously, we were enduring Bob's attempt at playing God.

As Dad queued waiting to turn right, I noticed there was a man at the bus stop reading the local evening paper; our story on the front page. If only he knew that the person he was reading about was looking at him, wondering what he was thinking as he read the unfolding drama.

Feeling strangely resentful of this man's normal life, I brought myself back to wondering how Junior would react to my battered appearance. I knew that before I would be able to hug Junior once more I would have to convince Social Services that Junior would be safe with me, his mum who has always protected him until yesterday. What a failure; I knew I had let him down badly. Would I ever be able to make it up to him?

After two and a half hour's of questions, statements and wrangling I was allowed to take Junior home. Not to our home; that was no more an option. To my mum's, Junior's second home. The whole process reminded me I now had the label of 'Victim' stamped across my forehead. I dutifully took on the title once more.

As we entered the locked security doors of the hospital wing I gasped as I saw Junior approaching the double doors expectantly. He looked so normal, yet how could he be? My love for him was so overwhelming I had to stop myself breaking down and running to him. 'Be strong Al' my dad said. 'He doesn't want to see you upset, you have to be strong for Junior's sake.' Of course he was right, so not for the first time, I stood as straight as I could, smiled and pushed down my emotions of pain.

'Mummy, you're hurt!... I've been on a bike, can I come home now?'

'Of course love.' Scooping him up, stick in one

hand, we had the best hug ever.

But getting Junior in the car was not a pleasant experience; he kicked and punched as the memory of being forcibly carried and pushed into the car by Bob a day earlier came into his mind. Holding him tight and reassuring him that he was safe did nothing to allay his fears. This was to be the first of many flashbacks Junior experienced over the next few years. My baby boy was not coming home the same Junior, he was gone.

We were welcomed home by a bed of flowers on my parents' drive and cards from friends and well-wishers waited in the porch. Rather than bringing joy and comfort from their well-meant gestures, I couldn't help but think it looked like the day of a funeral. It could have been our funeral day.

Placing Junior on the 'At Risk' register was another stab at my conscience and pain. Surely they could see I was a good mother, but seeing wasn't enough, they had to ask people who knew me or knew of me, friends, the Sikh shop owners who so kindly tended to me, Nigel and his partner, the list was endless. My life was laid bare for all to see and enquire; no privacy for me now.

I passed the test, Junior and I could stay together

as long as we lived with my parents until I was 'well enough'. My mental state was not classed as stable as signs of post-traumatic stress started to appear.

The long road to recovery was nowhere in sight. The first few days with Junior home were challenging on so many levels. I couldn't relate to him after our initial reunion; he reminded me of his dad, the man I had grown to hate. Thankfully this didn't last too long, Mum and Dad were amazing, adopting roles as secondary parents.

The head of the nursery was an incredibly inspirational help to us in the early days. Mrs Jones visited us at my parents' to state her support and suggested that Junior needed normality; it would make him feel safe and secure. So against my initial wishes to keep him close to me I took him back to nursery, his constant in his life at that time.

This was fantastic advice as Junior started to thrive once more; it was the nights that were difficult. The first few nights, he insisted on sleeping with me. As he was awoken by flashbacks of his recent ordeal he lashed out and punched me right on the mouth where my lips had previously been stitched back together.

He was also aware that mummy's hearing wasn't

the same; it still hadn't returned. I started to lip read to make out what people were saying, or I relied on my family to interpret for me. A trip to the GP was inconclusive; he offered me his condolences but that was it. My hearing would return I was assured, yet again.

After a few broken nights, Junior and I were exhausted. We both retired to bed at the same time so I could attempt to sleep. As exhaustion kicked in, I fell into a deep, fitful sleep, then I was awoken by Junior telling me there was a fire in our room.

A large basket of clothes that had been collected earlier from our old home had been placed directly under a strip light. Junior and I could no longer bear the dark of night, so I would leave the light on. After a few hours, unbeknown to us, the clothes were touching the light and had started to smoke and smoulder. Junior woke me just in time as the flames started to build.

After dousing the fire, we returned to bed and slept; this wasn't a drama to us after the recent events. The following day I was due to go back to our former home to collect the rest of my belongings.

Gail, my school friend of seventeen years was to come with me. The letting agency informed me that my belongings had to be collected, otherwise I wouldn't get my £400 deposit back. I instructed them to get the house cleaned up so we would not have to face it, but they didn't. Gail offered to help me instead. I could not allow my family to see the residue of the attack, I had to protect them from that, but Gail assured me she could cope.

As we entered my former home, Junior safely at nursery, the horror was still there. My hair was wrapped around the door catch and finger marks of blood trailed from the living room. Walking past the kitchen, the spag bol was still in the pan, gas off.

As we entered the scene of the crime, we were horrified to see it in its original state. Blood had oozed into the carpet creating a permanent pattern. There was blood on the walls, and Junior's potty was full! Chairs were knocked over and the actual area in the corner where I was straddled was clearly evident for Gail to witness.

Visibly shocked and abhorred, Gail tried her best to hide her feelings. She knew she had to be strong for me. I couldn't protect her as I had started to protect my other loved ones. So, practical as ever, Gail proceeded to clean the walls of my blood.

Gail told me years later on her deathbed – cancer

was her attacker – that she had hated what she saw and what she had to do. I wholly apologised and begged her forgiveness. Of course she had already forgiven me. A true friend.

Black bags packed, door locked, never to return there again. That was our life in bags.

A few days later, Gail was again asked to help me out. Mum and Dad needed to get away for some respite from the situation, and asked Gail to babysit. Not Junior, me.

By now I had become increasingly erratic, convinced Bob was going to send someone to finish the job and return to kill us both. I would repeatedly check on Junior, check the locks, windows, constantly moving round the house, not able to sit still.

'God you look a bloody mess' Gail said. 'And you stink! When did you last wash?' Well, what was the point in washing? What did I have to wash for? Where had the Alison gone who used to spend hours preening, washing, moisturising? She had gone.

Kicking me into action, Gail really pissed me off. 'How dare she tell me I stink, does she not know I am a VICTIM?' I thought. 'Who does she think she is? 'Everyone else is looking after me, fussing over me.' It did the trick though. Up the stairs I went, shower on, shampoo and soap.

A cleaner and grateful me returned to a warm loving hug. I felt very blessed to have such great friends and family.

The next day was another day of questions, interrogations and photos. The police had decided that waiting three days after the attack was enough. Now in our new home, my mum and dad left us to it. Louise insisted on being there for the questioning and was surprised how I 'protected' Bob. I didn't give the full facts initially, odd as it may sound I felt disloyal. Mad I know, this man had tried to take our lives and I was holding back with the full force of the truth. I was also totally ashamed and embarrassed. The truth of his reign of terror was now outed. Strangely, I felt responsible.

As Louise left the photographer arrived. The two male CID men told me they needed shots of my wounds. I thought they would just take photos of my face, visibly now healing incredibly well. 'No, we need you to take your top off... and your bra.' There were no female police officers there and my mum was in the back room. Remember, I was now fully in the role of victim and victims do as they're told, so off came my top, and then off came my bra.

Flashes of light were followed by merciless teasing about the size of my breasts. The officers felt it was appropriate to take advantage of this female victim and poke fun at the breasts that due to their size saved my life.

This was our secret and was to stay that way for a while. The shame of victimhood was building up all around me and I was helpless to it.

I was informed that Bob was now in the local prison and had been formally charged with two counts of attempted murder. He'll get ten years I was told.

This turned out to be not quite the case – thirteen months later at Crown Court, Bob was sentenced to three years' imprisonment for 'administering a noxious substance with intent to endanger life'. His charges for the attack on me were 'put on paper'. He spent half of his sentence in an open prison where his probation officer informed me he got fit.

There were many other situations that occurred, but are quite simply too exhausting to detail; lack of information, Bob being granted bail in Devon then flouting the conditions and frequenting my local area, being able to make telephone calls to our home to further the torment, the list goes on.

Wasn't I brave mummy?

A while after The Awakening, I'm not sure when, I was driving Junior to a party. He was sitting in the back in his car seat. As we were driving along we would naturally chat about different things; it was always agreed by Carl and my family that if Junior asked any questions about the attack or if he simply wanted to talk about it, we would stop what we were doing and listen to him, answering any questions openly and honestly without bad-mouthing Bob. After all he was still his father.

We knew we had to take away the hugeness of the events to help Junior's recovery too.

So there we were driving along this one day and Junior said to me 'you know Mummy, I was very brave I was' as only children can speak. And of course I answered 'You're always brave, Junior'.

'No mommy, when Bob did that to me I was really brave.' And as always when he mentioned Bob's name or the attack, my stomach would lurch and my heart would feel as if it was breaking into a million pieces followed by a huge sense of mourning. Mourning of the events and what they brought to our lives.

Composing myself, I said 'why were you so brave, Junior?' 'Well Mummy, when he took me in the car after he hurt you with a knife, he pushed me down by the front seat' (meaning the footwell) 'and he covered me with a blanket, and I couldn't breathe. But I was really clever I was Mummy, because every now and again I would put my head up and take a few gulps of air and then he'd push my head back down and point the knife at me. But I knew Mummy to stay alive I had to take deep breaths.'

Out of the mouths of babes! That said it all. This taught me that not only have I got an incredibly brave, strong and courageous young man as a son, I believe we all have that strength within us, but sometimes we don't know where to find it or how to look for it.

Junior found it, and that's what kept him alive. As I'm writing this, we've just celebrated Junior's nineteenth birthday, and he is a confident, handsome, 6 foot tall man who has a strong foundation in life with strong views, and who is determined in everything he does. So I'm glad Junior found that strength and continued to find strength. If you are reading this and you don't know where to look for your strength, rest assured you will find it, just keep looking and keep asking for help. If it is your child who is struggling, be open and honest and consistent with your love; and they will find their strength.

I'm sure you're wondering what happened to Carl. Well how it all happened is a blur. He returned from Europe a few days earlier than planned. When he had heard what happened he wanted to travel straight home but Jackie quite rightly suggested he continue his trip and return when things had settled down.

I wasn't really thinking of Carl and our future; I had too many other things to consider, getting Junior help for instance, answering his continual questions – 'why did Daddy want to kill us?'

The day before my birthday, 11th September 1994, Jackie insisted I came out with the biker group at least for an hour or two. It wasn't easy leaving Junior; he wanted to be with me the whole time when he wasn't at nursery. Not that I wanted to go out particularly, but I must admit a couple of hours away from the situation was appealing.

Upon entering the local pub, Carl was awaiting my arrival. It was a lovely surprise to see him although his appearance had altered somewhat; he was very tanned and wore a thick beard. Now I'm not a fan of facial hair, but in this case an exception was made.

I had to try and compose myself when seeing Carl as he was a reminder of what my life used to be like... before the attack as I kept calling it; now aptly named The Awakening.

As we sat together, the story poured out, yet I was becoming aware that I didn't want him to be upset or disturbed. I had realised a few weeks earlier that I had adopted a new survival technique, which was to try and protect my loved ones' feelings – insisting I was fine and getting over it, yet inside I was in complete turmoil.

Visibly shaken Carl tried to comfort and reassure me, but I moved away as he tried to hug me; I wasn't ready for that.

When I recall all my friends and family who loved and supported us at that time, my heart fills with gratitude: my brother and his wife – she was able to connect with me in a way that no one else could as she had experienced her own trauma years before;

Louise and Ken, the constant support. (Louise's pregnancy went overdue. They put it down to stress!)

Jackie, Gail and Jessie, another school friend who insisted I stayed with her at her family home for two weeks when I was too scared to leave my parents convinced Bob would send someone to kill us; at least he wouldn't know we were at Jessie's was the logic. Last but not least, my mum and dad. Not once did they say 'we told you so'. I bless them for that.

Something was stopping my healing: me! I had torturing thoughts that I must be evil – well why else would something so evil happen? I didn't feel I deserved to be happy, to be a mum, friend, sister, daughter. What could I give? All my thoughts and beliefs had been stripped away from me; my life bare for the world to see and interrogate. 'She's the girl who was stabbed' I would hear. One lady asked me what it was like to be stabbed. 'Fetch me a knife and I will show you' was my now cold reply. My foundations stripped, I later used this to create a new me with new foundations, but it took me years to embrace that thought.

Secretly I would plot how I was going to leave this life, then my selfish thoughts would be overrun by my ever-stronger maternal feelings towards Junior. I had to make it up to him somehow. To compensate I tried to be the best mum I could.

Our new home

After just over two months at mum and dad's, I decided with Social Services approval that we were to move into a small flat nearby. If I stayed with them any longer I was convinced that I would never be able to leave, as I so heavily relied and depended on their love and support. Junior now had two extra parents as opposed to grandparents and he loved it. My money was saved and the day of the move appeared; along with the rain. One of my dad's friend insisted on helping us by supplying a van and men without any charge. Aren't people amazing when help is needed?

After a few weeks we settled in quite well. Junior would stay at his Nan and Grandad's on a Friday night so I could go out with my friends and resume a normal life. Carl and I were now an item and very much in love; even with all the difficulties still remaining. I don't know how we did it. We slowly introduced Carl into Junior's life at Junior's pace and with my family's blessing.

We spent Christmas Day together and had real fun for the first time in months. Carl had bought me a car and presented the keys to me on Christmas night. Overwhelmed with his kindness, words left me.

But just as I was beginning to relax into some kind of normality, all the emotions I had been holding in, the protection I had built up for others, started to crack. I had bouts of real depression and lethargy that would grip me and debilitate me.

I was still allowing myself to be a victim. Sometimes petrified to leave the flat I would run to the local shop with my head down so as not to be recognised. Once when Junior and I were doing our laundry at the local laundrette, I heard someone shout my name; it was one of Bob's friends and I immediately felt we were being threatened. Grabbing the wet washing we ran home, locking and bolting the door behind us.

Just over a year later Carl and I bought our first home together. Junior loved it, being a unit with his mum and 'Carl Daddy' as he now called him.

The night traumas and flashbacks continued. Junior would wake every night, I would go in and comfort him, then It was my turn to have flashbacks and Carl would comfort me. This was our life for about three years. Carl then had to get up at 4am to go to his driving job. Exhausting!

We tried to keep life as normal as possible; trouble was, we didn't know what normal was.

Carl would often sit me down at our old pine table when Junior was in bed or playing with his toys. 'You're going to help people. Many people' he would say. 'I can see you.' Carl was convinced; his prediction was to be confirmed a few years later.

A couple of months after our move, we then we had the most amazing news; I was pregnant with twins! A cause for celebration.

Weeks later a miscarriage meant there was now one. Stress, I was told.

Our new life

Carl and I married on 8th March 1996, I was thirty-four weeks pregnant and proud! We knew we would be married, it was just a matter of time. After several discussions and no formal proposal I decided to take matters into my own hands. It was Carl's thirty-sixth birthday and his beloved football club were playing at home. That was how he wanted to spend his birthday so who was I to argue? I was heavily pregnant and feeling it; my evening was to be spent with Gail reminiscing and catching up with her gossip.

I confided in Gail that I had done something! Eventually I confessed that in a moment of madness I had telephoned the football club and asked if they would make an announcement to Carl Ward at half time. 'Of course that would be our pleasure' was the reply I received from the young customer service assistant. 'There's something else I want you to add please; would you also ask Mr Ward if he would marry his girlfriend Alison?' The girl couldn't contain her excitement.

Now Carl is a private person, to have this announcement made in public must have been so embarrassing for him, to have it made at the footie ground… well he admitted later he loved it. When the announcement was made his brother and friends pointed to him so the home fans could see the victim. He called me from his mobile to say 'yes'.

Family complete

Our son, David was born on a beautiful spring

afternoon, Friday 19th April 1996. Carl was with me, holding my hand and helping me through the whole birth, all four hours of it. Easy! Well in comparison to Junior's birth it was.

Carl helped make the birth a wonderful experience for all of us. After David entered the world, Carl collected Junior from school so he could see his new baby bro! I remember looking out of the hospital window watching them walk towards the hospital – well, Carl walked and Junior pulled him along in his eagerness to meet David.

Tears of joy fell down my face, and I felt immense pride for our new family and how far we had come, most of all I was so proud of Junior. He had to endure four house moves following The Awakening, starting school, having a new dad and a new brother and here he was eager to join in. What a star!

Motherhood the second time round was oh so different; I had the full loving support of a husband and fantastic dad, plus a son who was so thrilled at having a normal life. Things started to look up.

Junior continued to call Carl 'Carl Daddy' until one day when playing on the floor with his beloved dinosaurs, Junior said 'look Carl Daddy, what do you think of these, Daddy what do you think?' This was the first time Junior had dropped the Carl. Carl and I looked at each other without saying a word, tears pricked our eyes and an important discussion was raised.

'I want to adopt Junior Al.' By now I knew Carl well enough that if he said such a statement, he meant it.

Phone calls were made and an appointment at a city solicitors told us that I would also have to adopt Junior even though I was his birth mother. We were also informed that we were not entitled to full legal aid. Carl was a driver; the wages weren't grand by any means. Still it was important to us and where we wanted our family to go. Bob or 'Junior's natural father' as we now called him was classed as a category A offender and a risk to children after being found guilty of 'administering a noxious substance with intent to endanger life'. Ironically, Bob after being informed of our family's plans, contested the adoption and got full legal aid.

Thirteen months later and thousands of pounds in debt we successfully adopted Junior after lengthy and upsetting legal representations by Bob, meaning we had to attend family court on almost a weekly basis. He was able to use the system to continue his torment of abuse until one day, 24th June 1997, when an experienced and empathetic judge declared that enough was enough for our family. He urged Bob to back down and release his contestation. Adoption granted.

A few weeks previous to this, Carl and I were exhausted; we had endured thirteen months of financial hardship, an ever-growing debt to fund the adoption, we had a child who still didn't sleep through, plus Junior who although was happier was still experiencing flashbacks and some behavioural problems.

After another painful court session where Bob's representation was playing for time, Court was adjourned and I was summoned to have a discussion with the three solicitors and court guardian. 'Alison we feel it would be a good idea if you and Bob had a meeting. Maybe you could get him to drop the contestation.' At first I considered it to be an absurd idea, and then quickly realised it was the only way to adopt Junior and fully move on.

The meeting was set, nerves abound, stomach in knots I entered the small room. Before entering, I asked my grandad who was in spirit, (remember, he was on the welcoming committee in the tunnel of transition) to help me. 'Give me courage and strength please Grandad.' The reply was immediate, I felt him, he was with me in a flash.

The small room was dark, without natural sunlight, clearly representing our moods. There was a desk-like table in the centre with a chair on each side facing each other. The room was lined with solicitors, Junior's court Guardian and no one else.

This was the first time I saw Bob close up since that day in 1994, straight away I was back there, time warped in my little lounge and he was preparing to launch his attack. 'Aargh, I can't do it, I just can't do it' I thought, but as I turned my back to release myself from this room and my attacker, a cloak of strength and pure determination engulfed me. Turning round to face the father of my son, I took a deep breath of courage and stared him right in the face, sitting down I then expressed a statement, my eyes not leaving his:

'You will respect me as I have respected you by allowing this meeting to take place. When I have finished, you will leave. Do you understand me?'

Bob nodded. Not acceptable. 'Do you agree?' My voice was sharper, more determined.

'Yes.' His reply was weak, giving me more strength.

I then related his former actions on that fateful day – evident to all, this was the truth they were hearing, details complete and intense. The look of horror in his eyes as he recognised my recollection of events was oh so sweet. Gasps from our audience added to my performance.

'I have finished, you may leave' I instructed; with a dismissive wave of my hand. Obeying, Bob got up and walked out of the room with his head bowed and his energy depleted and rejected. His fight was over and I was no longer a victim.

The solicitors joined as one and applauded me. 'I have never seen such strength of character in all my years of practice' exclaimed the Pit Bull, the nickname I had given to Bob's solicitor. 'Well done.'

I was patted on the back, my hand shaken until it trembled and tears of joy and release flowed. I was now free of him for the first time. The realisation that he could never hurt me and us, my family, again finally hit me and the relief was overwhelming.

I left the room a changed woman.

Collecting Junior from school that day was glorious. His teacher brought him over to us and asked for an update. 'We did it! We adopted Junior.' Applause and laughter ensued as the information leaked around the playground. 'I hope you're having some champagne' his teacher suggested. Funny, we didn't feel like celebrating. We went home, had tea and went to bed as a new family, exhausted but happy.

Junior chose his new name and started to practise his signature. 24th June was declared a family day; one which would be celebrated each year. Junior angled for an additional birthday. Nice try Junior, this is a family celebration. Accepting and happy Junior picked up his dinosaurs.

A week later, Junior was invited to visit the judge to ask any questions he may have. Armed with his new birth certificate and identity, we celebrated at Pizza Hut.

LESSONS LEARNT

- *Believe in miracles; they do happen, particularly when your life is in danger and it's not your time.*

- *Forgive self even more.*

- *Keep blue straws in the cupboard.*

- *Learn to ask for help; it lets the other person experience the gift of giving and teaches you the Spiritual Law of Giving and receiving; bringing balance to your life, even in extreme circumstances.*

- *Allow children to express themselves without judgement; they are the voice of our future.*

- *Be open with children; if they ask a question, answer it in TRUTH.*

- *Be consistent with children, particularly when a trauma or transition occurs. They feel safe knowing their boundaries.*

- *Allow guidance to come through by connecting to your breath each day.*

- *Call upon your deceased loved ones to help guide you in times of struggle and listen for their reply. Be open to receiving their reply in unexpected ways; a song on the radio, a thought, feelings of strength. Then thank them.*

Discovering A New Faith

With the dramas of the last three years or so over, one would think that life would settle down and a normality would take over. It did of sorts; Carl and I enjoyed family life, I was getting to the point where I was considering returning to work, and Junior was getting some professional help which thankfully was working.

Saying all this, I would often be overwhelmed with a deep, engulfing depression, where I felt unworthy, invisible and non-deserving of the love I received from Carl and my family. I would question why it happened, did I deserve it? Maybe I had some sort of devil in me that made it happen. Eventually, Louise came to my rescue with her forthright approach. 'Don't you think that bastard has ruined your life enough without him ruining it anymore?' Of course she was right. So why did I feel so low? I concluded that my family would be better off without me. Surely they would cope without me there, Carl's an amazing dad, he could meet someone else and she could be their mum.

You may think this sounds utterly selfish, maybe it does. All I know is that the years of torment, lack of sleep and stress had culminated in me feeling so desolate, so unreachable. Even Carl's talks at the famous pine table couldn't lift me.

Jessie popped round one time and whilst sharing a coffee she too tried to bolster my mood. 'Al, the best form of revenge is happiness!' True, a great way at looking at a negative situation, yet I just couldn't see the point of continuing. A trip to the GP resulted in tablets 'to help me' and an appointment with a psychiatrist was planned.

Junior had an amazing child psychologist after we ploughed through a few duff ones. She knew him, understood him and accepted him. Sitting with him as Junior played out the characters in *The Lion King*, he was fascinated by the story when Scar pushes his brother Mufasa over the cliff making him King. These sessions proved to be invaluable for Junior and his healing process. It was his time to be heard and he used it to express his fears and experiences following that fateful day.

Dr Moses encouraged Junior to draw, colour and write about his feelings. The pictures said a thousand more things than words ever could. It was the way forward and Junior started to blossom under this doctor's wing, just as colour was brought to his pictures, colour came into his life.

Although there were promising inputs, Junior and I still had flashbacks at night, quickly followed by panic attacks. Our routine took on almost a comical routine. I would wake up first, waking Carl up who would calm me down, assuring me I was safe, then I would drift back off to sleep, to be awoken by Junior. I then would attend to Junior, followed by David as he was awoken by the noise. Then at 4am Carl would be woken up by his alarm telling him it was time for work.

It was on one of those nights when again I was awoken by a flashback. It was like watching a movie of the attack, but I had no control over the pause or stop button. This time Carl didn't stir; poor man, he was probably exhausted. The movie got worse, followed by sweating, hyperventilating, crying and still Carl didn't stir. How could I go on like this I asked, surely it would be better to end my miserable life? Momentarily thinking what was the best and easiest method to commit suicide, I felt an unusual presence.

My angel appeared

Suddenly a beautiful presence appeared at my side of the bed. The room filled with light and still Carl didn't stir. Absurd as it may sound, I could clearly see an angel; I accepted what was unfolding. My angel, whom I later called Sarah, told me that I was safe; she stroked my arm with the gentlest of strokes and I could feel her touch. Never before had I seen an angel, but I believed in them for sure; if you had asked me what I would have expected my angel to look like I wouldn't have known the answer. What I can say with absolute honesty and integrity is she was beautiful. Her hair was the blondest, silkiest hair I had ever seen, her eyes the bluest of all oceans and her skin was luminescent, with no lines of stress or age. It shined as if light was pouring in from behind her face. I accepted her presence as if it was the most natural thing to occur in the middle of the night.

She continued; 'You are safe, it will never happen

to you and Junior again. We love you, you are safe...' The words I longed to hear and believe were being poured into me. God this was pure bliss. The love she gave to me in the gentlest of strokes and her simple presence was feeding me, nurturing me. This gift was the most incredible, powerful love I have ever experienced; even more than when you hold a newborn baby for the first time; there are simply no words to describe the experience.

The feelings of panic began to disappear, for the first time in years I was given peace. Peace – something we all take for granted at times, had eluded me for so long yet was now being given to me; the greatest gift ever. She continued 'you have great things to do here, remember you are safe, no harm will come to you now.'

As my demeanour softened, my heart opened and fear left me that night, never to return in full force again. Carl then started to stir, but still my angel spoke 'we love you, you are safe...'

'What the f**k is going on?' Carl was not used to seeing an angel in his bedroom talking to his wife!

'It's ok Carl, I'm ok.'

Getting up from the bed, Carl assumed he had awoken from a dream and duly went to the bathroom. Upon his return, he freaked out a little. 'Al someone's talking to you.'

'I know; it's ok Carl, we're going to be ok.' He then proceeded to tell me that he could hear other voices too; unpleasant voices calling me unpleasant names. He could not visibly see anything, only hear. Funny – I was aware of these other voices, but I was able to dismiss them without any effort. The love and strength given to us that night by my angel blanked out these lowly threats and was to sustain us forever. The lower voices soon left – beaten by the light we concluded later (after months of debating.)

Eventually the night settled down, and my angel left as gently as she arrived; a peaceful, unbroken night's sleep followed; the first in an age.

Never again was I to have a flashback or a suicidal thought. The recovery had clearly started; how could it not with my angel by my side, forever loving me, guiding and protecting me? No one could ever take that away from me. For the first time since the day of The Awakening I had a glimmer of hope – knowing I was not alone, that I was loved and safe changed my life forever.

In the next part of the book I share the tools and experiences that evolved after the evening I met my angel. As I found peace and faith, I discovered more tools that we all have but maybe don't always look for. These simple, yet affective practices were to add an extra element to my life; keeping fear at bay. Now, after seventeen years of writing this book, those fearful times have all but disappeared. The most amazing and inspiring, as well as empowering tool, I discovered was the gift of guidance or intuition. The following chapters clearly illustrate how my gift was awakened, developed and nurtured, by acting upon the guidance given – what a wonderful gift it has proven to be, helping me assist so many over the years.

Back to work

I returned to work in 1998 in a job I grew to love. I'd had two ear operations to correct my hearing so I was unable to commit to a regular job before then.

Now my outlook was more positive, I decided that each year on the anniversary of The Awakening I would create something new and positive; coincidental then, that 5th July 1998 was my first day working as a Volunteer Coordinator at a hospice.

In fact it was quite interesting how this job came

about. Louise was working in the fundraising department and she heard they were advertising the job of volunteer coordinator. She phoned me to say 'this job has got your name all over it, you need to apply.' Before having my children I had worked in recruitment. At first I dismissed working in the same work place as Louise and stubbornly said I wouldn't apply if she was 'to put a word in for me.' I had to get a job on my own merits.

The interview went well – I had a rapport with the Volunteer Manager and the job was offered to me and I accepted. A hospice is a wonderful place to work – yes it was sometimes sad when you heard of a death; patients often went there to live their final days, as well as having some respite care when they were battling a terminal illness. But there was also lots of laughter and lots of fun. Every day was to make a difference to everyone; staff and patients alike. I met some really beautiful people there and some cherished memories were formed.

Working there taught me a huge amount about people; in fact I see that experience as a steep learning curve for me in my life so far. It was quite obvious working there, that complementary therapy was starting to be accepted by the conventional medical world. As I progressed and settled in, I was asked to help develop a team of complementary therapists headed by a nurse, Jan, who was to become my Reiki Master Teacher at a later date. This was just heaven for me, working with like-minded people and developing the team was just fantastic. While this complementary scheme was being developed at the hospice I noticed the most popular therapy was Reiki. I then recalled Gail telling me about it in previous years. The wonderful thing about Reiki is that it is a totally non-intrusive treatment, there's no need to undress or get on a couch to receive it; you can stay in the bed or on a chair while the therapist gently places her hands on and around your body. Further research explained that Reiki channels the pure life force energy that is around every living thing. For it to really work effectively the therapist would have done some good self personal development work to enable them to open their heart and allow the loving energy to flow through them to the patient.

I often saw patients or their carers come out of the treatment room after they had a Reiki session; they look very relaxed and appeared much calmer than when they went in. I remember a lovely Birmingham guy, a typical down to earth working class man, who used to work at 'the Austin'. He would not accept that Reiki or other complementary therapies could help him. When I enquired if he had tried it, his reply was, 'I'm not having any of that stuff, its mumbo jumbo.' So seeing an opportunity to get another satisfied customer I suggested he had a go. Not wanting to be beaten, he did. I saw him going into his Reiki appointment muttering under his breath, then when he came out he said 'I don't know what she did to me, but I'm having some more of it next week!'

He received Reiki every week until he passed and it was wonderful to observe his changing behaviour. I saw his demeanour change from being angry at his disease and the consequences of it, to acceptance and being at peace. I was told he died peacefully, which helped his family and friends accept his passing. You could argue he would have died at peace anyway, but I truly believe Reiki helped him. That's what I love about Reiki; it's so loving and accepting. Anyone can do it as long as they are attuned by a Reiki master teacher.

Whilst I worked at the hospice I was still having some flashbacks and nightmares, as was Junior. My sister Louise suggested that I tried Reiki as there was a staff discount scheme. I decided to have a go. I went along to Jan's house – a beautiful terraced house about five minutes drive from the Hospice, where she had transformed a bedroom into a really safe and comfortable place to receive a multitude of therapies.

At the time it was about £25 per session, which was quite a lot of money to us, as we were still in debt from the adoption and court costs. But Carl and I recognised that this was an investment in my health and well-being which in turn would benefit us all. He insisted on picking me up after the treatment as he didn't want me to drive home – we weren't sure how I would react.

Straightaway I felt at ease with Jan, her years of experience as a nurse really helped in putting me at ease. In a nice warm room I got onto a very comfortable couch and was wrapped up with a blanket with some relaxing music on, and for the next 45 minutes Jan placed her hands upon my head and then my body, ending with my feet. It was a wonderful experience. As I closed my eyes I drifted into a slumber, which became deeper as the treatment progressed. I remember seeing a picture of a white eagle in my mind's eye, maybe it was a dream, who knows? This eagle looked at me, opened its wings to full span and then gently closed them again. I felt it was a sign of spiritual protection and I knew I was in a safe place. I also knew that this was the beginning of my healing process; to be normal once more. Whatever normal is!

Jan placed her hand on my shoulder. 'Alison, gently come round.' I was startled at how relaxed I felt. For the first time in four years I felt a deep sense of peace; I was hooked.

Jan prepared me by advising to take it easy and be gentle with myself for the next few days. It was a Friday evening so advised me not to have any alcohol or spicy foods, but to have a nice early night so the effects of the Reiki would stay with me longer. I decided to follow this advice as all I wanted to do was get into bed, snuggle up and go to sleep. I phoned Carl after leaving Jan's house to say I was ready to be collected, and eventually he found the house, it was quite difficult to understand me as I was in a somewhat relaxed state. He found it quite amusing. When we got home I said I wanted an early night, and off I went. The next day was a Saturday, with the normal family chores that happen at a weekend – cleaning, cooking, shopping, taking

Junior to football, looking after David (who was now two years old), a typical busy weekend. Imagine my surprise when instead of feeling really chilled and relaxed, anger started to rise within me, I had felt this anger rising many times since The Awakening, but I always used to push it down. It wasn't going to be pushed down today. As it welled up within me, I felt it was going to burst open at any moment. It did.

As soon as Carl returned home from work, I started uncharacteristically yelling, shouting, smashing plates, screaming. I blamed Carl for what Bob did to Junior and me, I accused him of leaving us as sitting ducks – 'if you hadn't gone to Europe on that day, it never would have happened.' Of course that wasn't the truth, but somewhere within me I felt part of it was the truth; I found myself blaming Carl for not protecting us from the atrocities of that day. Which was untrue, it was going to happen, no matter what. Bob had every intention of killing us that day and fate dropped in to prevent it from happening.

The angry torrent continued for the rest of the weekend; words, ugly words, tumbled out of my mouth directed at Carl and I honestly thought my marriage was over. The tears and sobs that wracked my body meant I was a wreck when Monday morning arrived. I don't know how I got to work on that day but I did. By then the decision was made; I was never going to have Reiki again.

Walking into the Hospice I saw a familiar friendly face, Sue, one of the senior therapists, who also was a nurse, and another therapist Pam. Seeing the state of my swollen eyes, they asked me what was wrong. I poured out to them how I felt and how I was never going to have this 'voodoo Reiki' again, how it probably had wrecked my marriage... the list went on.

'Congratulations, you've had what we call a healing crisis. It won't happen again but because you've been holding onto this anger for so long, and because the Reiki is an intelligent energy it has helped you release it. Alison, you're working in a hospice. If you look around you will notice that some people are here because they have held onto anger and past hurts and it has festered within them creating the cancer, not all, but some.'

I knew she was right, for I had spoken to those patients and they had shared that with me. In fact in the years that followed when Gail passed with cancer, she also accepted that it had grown within her, due to her bitterness and upset at her marriage ending. So I knew at some level that Pam and Sue were right in what they were saying, but I was just so exhausted. Tired and worn out like a wrung out towel, I was determined not to have Reiki again. But Sue insisted. 'Please Alison, for you and your well-being, please book another treatment and go back.' I trusted both Sue and Pam, I knew they were both telling the truth and speaking from their hearts. I was able to recognise that even amongst all the bleariness of the pain I had received, endured and given out over the weekend.

I returned to Jan and Reiki the following week to receive another treatment, albeit a little wary, nervous and anxious. Meeting Jan, I shared the stories of the last week and she more or less repeated the same things that Sue and Pam had said to me. I lay on the couch and I again fell into a deep slumber. I noticed that when Jan's hands were on the back of my head, my head would start to pop as if pockets of energy were being released – it was very reassuring, it felt as if I was actually releasing nuggets of pain and I welcomed the popping. That was the beginning of my Reiki journey.

I continued to have regular treatments and became calmer and more accepting as a result; no longer seeing life as a drama. It was at this time I also started to practice working with Gratitude; combining it with mirror and acceptance work; all tools I was to be shown through receiving guidance.

Since that new beginning and even with events that have followed, I now always have peace, no matter what is going on around me. Sometimes I simply sit and connect to that peace within. I continue to practice Reiki and self-healing and remain in peace as a result; it never leaves me.

The tools of gratitude and acceptance

It is imperative that I talk about Gratitude, for gratitude was paramount in my continual healing and acceptance of who I was, helping to restore me to mental well-being once more. It helped me see The Awakening as a tragic event that no longer had a detrimental effect on my life. I was now able to view the effect of the event as a beautiful gift in an ugly box.

Gratitude helped me discover me again, releasing me from life's dramas, bringing with it a sense of renewed power. The day after the angelic meeting,

I woke to a new day with hope and a new way of living; of thinking, believing and, most of all, having faith.

This new lease of life helped me open the doors to discover the tools that lay within me. One of the first tools I found was Acceptance: to bring myself to look in the mirror and accept what was looking back at me. At first I experienced distaste, dislike and at times near hate, then I moved on to looking, seeing my reflection, liking it, and then to loving that reflection, and eventually onto acceptance of me.

Part of that development occurred due to gratitude, and I knew that for me to recover fully I had to discover hope and gratitude. I soon realised that expressing gratitude was the ingredient needed to re-discover hope. So as each day would pass, I would say thank you for the day, my life, my family's lives and health etc. Then I would express real gratitude for something specific before retiring to bed; I simply could not settle until actual gratitude relating to our life was expressed, closing the day.

I remember one evening pacing the bedroom floor while Carl was in bed waiting for me to join him – 'will you please come to bed?'

'I can't come yet, I haven't got anything to be

grateful for,' I exclaimed. After a particularly trying, exhausting day, I was finding it extremely challenging to be in gratitude. It was then I remembered that David, my baby, had filled a nappy. He had previously had an upset tummy; so while this nappy was filled with proper poo I was able to announce my absolute gratitude, feel it and end my day with gratitude.

As my acknowledgement of gratitude further developed it was also apparent that it needs to be expressed upon awakening on each morning. This was something that I truly tried to resist; was this ego? On the low days, when my eyes opened and I realised another day was before me, I often had a feeling of dread, doom and darkness. So for me to be guided to find gratitude before even leaving my bed was a huge challenge I eventually managed to overcome. I'd start by being grateful for opening my eyes and seeing what was before me, I would show gratitude for hearing my child's cry. I was hugely grateful and full of gratitude for hearing birdsong. As the gratitude grew further, my days of hope returned after many months. I didn't fully realise that hope had fully returned until one morning, as I walked to the bathroom a 'light switch' of hope awoke within me. It was actually a physical feeling too. I stopped in my tracks, acknowledged that something felt different, realised it was the growth of gratitude that I had brought into my discipline of living, and as such hope returned.

The by-product of hope was peace of mind – coupled with hope, peace of mind was its companion.

That evening I shared this discovery with Carl, who as always accepted what I was saying without question. 'So does that mean we can plan things now?' he enquired. You see we didn't plan anything until that day because I was truly fearful that the planned day would not come about, still convinced Bob would return to kill me or us. So you can see what gratitude brought to our lives.

This inner strength and discipline of integrating the gratitude practice, enabled hope and peace to be an integral part of our daily life.

There were days when it wasn't easy, in fact many times it would have been easier to stay a victim, where others would have tended to my needs, made my decisions. It was pure commitment and discipline that brought me back to myself, plus the loving support of my family and friends and of course my angel's presence.

The next stage was to listen to the words I used;

I no longer wished to use victim language, blaming others for example or saying the classic, 'it always happens to me.' When I used the word 'should', I would correct myself as it indicates that you're doing something that you would rather not, maybe you felt guilty if you didn't, pressure from others too often resulted in the word 'should' being used. I found my voice and found truth in the words I used, this was often quite challenging to some. Carl would often say, 'you don't let me get away with anything.' Always in good humour, he was relieved to have this stronger woman back.

As the healing developed, I felt like a new person, more confident and positive and noticed that I was attracting more positive situations in my life including lovely, uplifting people. The past was being left behind.

A light returned to my life with the help of Reiki and the wonderful support of my Reiki master, therapists and of course friends and family. I knew that I had to learn this healing art of Reiki so I could also practise and pass on the teachings to others. I knew I was meant to be a teacher. So for the next two years I was taught Reiki in a small group by Jan and fellow Reiki master, Pat. To me it was a very natural step. It reawakened the healing abilities I had as a child and developed them with integrity and discipline. To keep the Reiki energy in flow it's encouraged to self-heal twice a day – upon awakening and at the close of the day, when gratitude for the day has been expressed. This continues and aids a healthy sense of well-being. My nights became more peaceful, the nightmares still occurred, but the rawness of them was reduced by me applying Reiki whenever they happened; I had become empowered by using tools that worked.

I was also taught how to practise on others; my family, in particular Junior and David and often Carl. Junior was prone to having ear infections and would call out in the middle of the night with the pain, many a time I would sit on his bed and place my hands over his ears allowing the healing energy of Reiki to work its magic. Eventually he would drift off to sleep. I remember one morning, after seeing all the gunk from the ear infection on his pillow, Junior awoke feeling well once more; all without painkillers and antibiotics. Of course we had taken him to the doctors to get medication as I was trained that it's to be used alongside and in partnership with conventional medicine; complementary therapy complements mainstream medicine. Having Reiki in my life, and passing it on to my family and friends has acted as a glue of love helping us maintain balance and well-being within ourselves and our family.

As with all families and life, we still have our ups and downs but Reiki is always the glue, the thread that keeps the calmness and the peace.

When I completed my training I had a small group of people urging them to teach me. They knew I had been learning and practising now for nearly three years and were not put off by my lack of teaching experience. So while the ink was still drying on my certificates I began to teach my first group. It was so natural to me; I had found my calling, my purpose.

I continued teaching and practising and started a little business whilst still working at the Hospice. Knowing that at some point this would be my main work, I contacted the Inland Revenue and registered my business.

I also came up with the idea of running a Reiki clinic at the Hospice on a voluntary basis so I could 'give back'. Two nights a week after work, I would treat nurses and staff, placing any donations into the Hospice collecting box. My sense of satisfaction continued to grow, as did my gratitude for this wonderful life changing energy.

It soon became obvious that I couldn't keep working the hours; working at the Hospice as well as developing my business. Remember, I had a young family, a home, a husband and a dog that all needed my time. It was reaching a point when a decision had to be made; it was soon made for me. My life became busier and more hectic trying to fit everything in. I began to lose that peacefulness that Reiki had brought to me and taught me the art of being; I was too busy doing.

My body started to react to this busy-ness; vertigo appeared one morning and stayed with me for six months. It was a fast spinning sensation, accompanied by nausea, and I often had periods off work, unable to drive or even walk in a straight line. My trips to the GP resulted in being told it would go of its own accord. Six months later I was still feeling sick and dizzy, day-to-day events were extremely difficult to carry out. I had my final ear operation around this time and still the dizziness continued. It wasn't until I decided to look at what my body was trying to tell me that I got my answer. I asked my body 'what is going on with you? Why are you so dizzy?' The answer I got was, 'Alison you're out of balance and your body's reacting, things have got to change.'

I shared this discovery with Carl, and we decided that I couldn't maintain the hours I was working as well as run the house. So upon my return to work I reduced my hours to four days a week, swiftly reduced to three.

Leap of faith

A year or so later I was sitting in my office at the Hospice, eating an apple and looking at a piece of art given to me as a gift from a lovely volunteer. It was a painting of a Greek Island; I love the Greek Isles and have been to most of them. This volunteer thought the painting would remind me of my favourite place and help me if I was having a hard day. Chomping away at the apple and gazing longingly at the picture, I asked out loud, 'Angels please tell me when I should take a leap of faith and leave the Hospice.' I knew the time was near; my business had grown even more and I was once again struggling to fit it all in. I needed some confirmation to give me that final push. No sign was forthcoming so I continued to chew at my apple and lose myself in the Greek Island. It was then I noticed the artist's name, Angel. Was that a sign?

The next day I handed in my notice with Carl's blessing and I've never looked back. The last eight years since leaving the Hospice have taught me more about faith and belief than at any other time. There is a process of adjustment in being self-employed but with my renewed confidence and absolute belief in my abilities, we have continued to be provided for.

Angel therapy and Gail's passing

As my journey progressed, confidence and the business grew. I added more skills to the toolbox: crystal therapy, counselling skills, meditation etc. I knew that something else was needed to get me on the next step of the ladder. My intuition, guidance or inspiration, call it what you will, was really starting to develop; I began to trust it and ask for help when I needed guidance.

One day I was just browsing the web and came across an announcement that Doreen Virtue, the world-renowned expert on Angels and Angel Therapy was holding her first practitioner's course in Glastonbury in May 2005. The course was about one thousand pounds. I knew I had to go on it; my body started to tingle and a warm feeling filled my heart; things I had now recognised as clear signs that this was the right thing to do. Before I knew it, I entered my credit card details and pressed the send button. I had to wait two days to find out if I was accepted on the course.

I couldn't contain my excitement as I rang my mum to tell her. 'Guess what Mum...' She was thrilled and agreed it was definitely the right step. Telling Carl was more of a challenge as I hadn't told him before booking it; £1000 is a lot of money when you have a family. He thought it was a great idea, especially when I said it was a business investment and I would get the money back over the years.

Well, I had an amazing week in May 2005; Doreen Virtue is a beautiful lady inside and out. I remember wanting to get on the front row so I was outside the building at 7am; the course wasn't due to start until nine. When she walked into the room Doreen brought with her a truly beautiful presence. I felt very blessed being there.

Our last day was a trip to Stonehenge at five in the morning on a cold and drizzly day. I was not impressed! The American ladies were so in awe of the sacred place, many of them danced around amongst the stones. All I wanted to do was go home and sleep. I wasn't in the best of moods!

Imagine my surprise when I was introduced to a new gift. Leaning against a stone, I got out my notepad and sarcastically asked for the stones to give me a message. Was I losing the plot?

'You have healed all that you can for now. Embrace life for all that it is to you. Enjoy and surround yourself with love and joy.

'Plenty to go round. This stone represents unity of Godliness in you and every being who rests here. Find your Godliness and settle it within.

'Release your limitations and fly with LOVE.'

Reading back the hastily scrawled message I've got to admit I was gobsmacked. They were not my words, my thoughts. Excitement grew as I then asked for a message for the UK; what do you ask a stone who starts communicating with you??

'It's time to put down weapons – emotional weapons of destruction. Unity is the key. Join with the moon and stars and find your way home. Peace is within – you don't have to look too far.

Eat and re-cycle nature but keep it light – light in energy and essence. Eat light and be filled with light.

The stones have eyes – they are transmitting to the planet from whence they came.'

I was on a roll, not wanting this two-way conversation to end, I asked for a message to pass on to the people whom I would help. This is what was given:

'The gateway to heaven is there in your heart,

You have the key should you want to depart.

Follow the signs that are before you now,

Life will evolve, don't worry how.

You're not alone on a mountain top

But close to the heart that will never stop.

God is within you

Release him now.

Praise him and worship him, remember how?

Open your heart to his presence within.

Stop and be still child

And let it all in.'

To say I was blown away was an understatement; these were definitely not my words. I have since passed them on many times to people whom I've helped and they have given them comfort.

Although my experience on Doreen's course was truly inspiring and amazing in so many ways, it was tainted by a huge sadness. Gail, my school friend of twenty plus years, was now dying of terminal cancer. I begged her not to pass whilst I was away and she insisted I still went along. It had now been booked for twelve months, four months before Gail was diagnosed.

My friend was to pass two weeks after I returned home. Due to my newly-developed channelling abilities, I was able to give Gail the greatest of gifts.

I went to visit Gail three days before she died. She was now in a Hospice, in the Crystal room. How apt; I gave her crystal therapy many times over the last few months to help her cope with pain and nausea.

The visit was incredibly upsetting and also very beautiful. Gail confided in me that she was really affected by the time she cleaned my blood from the walls of the lounge where the attack took place and the clumps of hair from the handle and lock. She needed to share and release that with me and I accepted her pain. In return, I was able to give her a wonderful message from her angels.

Her sight had now failed and it was clear her time

was near; I asked her angels to draw close to me give Gail a message. The message was quickly written down through using me as channel. As I relayed this message to Gail, she started to cry, and I assumed they were tears of sadness. Gail corrected me to say 'no, they were tears of joy.' She said 'I thought they had left me,' meaning her angels. They had never left her; they were very much with her.

Gail's message was personal to her; I have no memory of the content. All I know is it gave her reassurance, comfort and love, and the most wonderful gift I could ever give to Gail also gave me comfort in return. There wasn't anything else I could do for her, I couldn't take away her pain, I couldn't give her any more energy to keep her alive, but I was able to give her this message of truth and love from her angels.

On the Friday evening, the eve of her death, I asked my friends and family to light a candle for Gail at 9pm and join together with our love and prayers. We had a wonderful vigil at home; Carl, Junior, David and I all lit a candle and expressed our thanks to Gail. We then hugged and sat and watched the candle flicker.

I was to witness a wonderful thing happening

just before Gail passed: I was at home feeling very, very tired, so I announced that I was going upstairs for a lie down. I was planning to see Gail later with another of her friends, Claire, but a part of me knew I wasn't going to see her alive again.

As I lay down on the bed I called upon Archangel Azrael to help Gail; I knew she was struggling and in pain. Azrael, I had discovered was the angel you call on when someone is dying. He helps with the transition, leaving this life and moving to our resting place.

As I pleaded with Azrael to help her, an outline of an angel appeared on the wall before me and next to the angel was a little girl with her arms outstretched. The angel picked up this little girl and flew off. You may suggest this was my imagination, that's what the logical part of me says, but the reality was I did actually see it.

Just then, the phone rang, loud crying hung in the background as her dad, Roger informed me that Gail had gone.

Sad yet determined to carry on, I have continued my work with renewed strength knowing that Gail is still around guiding me. I have felt her whilst writing this book, and at the suggestion of Junior, we have dedicated this book to Gail; bless you sweetheart.

LESSONS LEARNT

- *Surround yourself with loved ones, friends and uplifting people.*

- *Start asking for help; small steps to begin with.*

- *It gets easier after the initial ask.*

- *Believe in angels – they do exist.*

- *Find a job or purpose that matches your gifts and makes your heart sing, or indulge in a hobby that you enjoy.*

- *Use complementary therapy alongside conventional medicine. Recommendation is the best form of referral. Ask to see any testimonials, insurance documents and certificates.*

- *Do they belong to a professional body?*

- *Express Gratitude upon wakening and on retiring to bed.*

- *Look in the mirror and see you. Become your visual friend.*

- *Say 'I like you', progress to 'I accept you' whilst looking right at yourself.*

- *Listen to the signs, heighten your awareness and pay attention.*

- *Tell your loved ones and friends that you LOVE them.*

"Angel" Alison Ward

New Tools For The Toolbox

The angels send me to Dubai

At the end of 2006 I was sitting in my treatment room at home and as I normally do at that time of year, I gave thanks in meditation for the experiences of the past year. I am a great believer of showing gratitude as I believe it enhances the abundance energy and consequently acts in a snowball effect in other areas of life. As I sat there in silence and sent up my thanks, I then awaited instructions on what the forthcoming year would hold or what I was expected or being asked to do the following year. The sort of things I was expecting to hear were maybe, work with children more as during 2006 myself and a friend did some courses with children, teaching them about crystals and Reiki and energy; or maybe I would be asked to do some more with breast cancer patients; or do some more clinic work, that was really the sort of area I was expecting. Instead of instructions I was actually given: 'Well done, we praise and thank you for your hard work, it will pay off next year, 2007.' You can imagine this took me completely by surprise as I wasn't looking for any thanks. I was expressing gratitude for being shown ways that I could continue to serve using my gifts.

My logical side began to kick in and question what I'd heard. I asked the sort of questions that you may be asking now, such as: how do I know it's not my imagination? or, am I making it up? Either are quite valid questions – all I can say is I know the answer, I know when I hear and feel truth.

I then continued to tune in and listen for further instructions. I was given a message 'you must go to Dubai, you need to take the light to Dubai.'

Gobsmacked was an understatement! You could have knocked me down with an angel's feather! Dubai was not a place I ever intended to visit or even thought about.

I then questioned why Dubai should need more

light. (Surely not, it's a desert! Isn't it?) I thought it was a place of wealth, materialism, expectations, success. So why on earth would it need more light? This logical thinking, using the opposite side of the brain, promptly brought me out of meditation and I sat for a few moments questioning what I'd heard. I was totally bemused, trying to make sense of the message. As I sat there I knew then that it couldn't have been my imagination, it couldn't have been a seed placed there weeks, months, years before, because Dubai was simply a place I'd never thought of, or given any consideration to.

As I closed the meditation I sat for a few moments and wondered at this message, what a wonderful message, it didn't make much sense to me, but as I was digesting it and absorbing it I knew, I simply knew that there was a grain of truth starting to grow. I promptly walked into the living room where Carl, my husband, was watching TV and told him what had happened. We had now been together for fourteen years, and Carl was used to my strange ways. 'The angels want me to go to Dubai' I said, 'that's nice love' was my answer. All Carl wanted to know was when I'd be going and to make sure I gave him notice so he could take some time off to look after the boys. By this time David was 10 and Junior was 15.

After more pondering I remembered that my friend Mary's daughter, Liz had recently moved to Dubai, her husband had managed to get a three-year contract and they saw it as a new start of life. So I decided to give Mary a call. I had taught Mary Reiki a few years earlier and we had become friends.

After sharing the recent communication with her she expressed that it was a wonderful message. We continued to discuss it and both wondered what, if anything, would happen next. Just before the conversation came to a close we chatted about how wonderful it was to have Reiki, angels and the loving guidance they bring into our lives when unexpectedly a sentence poured out of my mouth without any thought; 'when you speak to Liz will you ask her if it's worth me coming over to Dubai to do some work there?'

I knew this was a pure channelled message, there was no thought or intention behind it. 'OK' Mary said, naturally accepting the question, 'I'll ring Liz tomorrow.'

The next evening a very excited Mary called me, 'Alison you'll never believe this. I've just spoken to

Liz and she's been to a Mind, Body, Spirit fair today in Dubai. She met someone who only knows you!' She kept repeating 'you won't believe it!' Well, by this point nothing came to me as a surprise, so I did believe it!

She then went on to say this person came to me for a reading and healing some years before and it helped her so much that she decided to develop her gift and she was now travelling around the United Arab Emirates working at the Mind, Body, Spirit fairs.

I just love coincidence and synchronicities, little miracles popping up everywhere reminding you you're on the right track. I wasn't overwhelmed by this new piece of information – I smiled knowingly; it was simply another piece of the jigsaw starting to slot into place.

Mary ended the conversation by saying 'Liz said you must come to Dubai, they need you.' The message was beginning to sink in. Maybe I was going to Dubai. When I saw Carl later I relayed this new piece of information. 'If you've got to go, you've got to go!' was his answer; he knew and understood my passion for my work, my purpose and had always supported and encouraged me, so it was decided that yes I would go to Dubai.

Shortly after, the ego decided to kick in; bringing with it the inevitable self-doubt which sadly is one of my old victim patterns. Who am I to go to Dubai? Why would they want me there? What have I got to give? I started to question the validity of the whole meditation experience again. What if I made it all up? Maybe it was my imagination? By now I had recognised my ego's reactions and was having none of it. What did I do? I opened my heart by imagining light and love pouring into it. Breathing deeply and smoothly my questions subsided and I felt peace return. I was then given this thought: 'Who are you not to go and shine your light?' I knew and felt that this was truth, it was now my truth. I decided to own it there and then and to take responsibility for it. I knew further enhancement of my life's journey was on the cards and I was up for it!

I must include a passage from Marianne Williamson here as it says it all:

Our Deepest Fear by Marianne Williamson

"Our deepest fear is not that we are inadequate. Our deepest fear is that we are powerful beyond measure. It is our light, not our darkness that most frightens us. We ask ourselves, Who am I to be brilliant, gorgeous, talented, fabulous? Actually, who are you not to be? You are a child of God. Your playing small does not serve the world. There is nothing enlightened about shrinking so that other people won't feel insecure around you. We are all meant to shine, as children do. We were born to make manifest the glory of God that is within us. It's not just in some of us; it's in everyone. And as we let our own light shine, we unconsciously give other people permission to do the same. As we are liberated from our own fear, our presence automatically liberates others."

When this episode of self-doubt passed I awaited more instructions and started to meditate in anticipation of the next jigsaw piece. I was further told there are many lost souls out there. Materialism has taken over from spirituality and the light has been blocked by greed creating these lost souls in need of LIGHT. I could feel further information stirring up and coming forward. Then to my surprise, amazement and utter glee, over the next four weeks four people who live and work in Dubai sourced me out for readings and spiritual guidance.

One of them was even on the way to the airport

and phoned me up to say 'I don't suppose you can fit me in can you?' Well I could and I did.

Surely that was another sign from my angels and spiritual team? Confirmation that this trip to Dubai was heaven sent.

One of the people, Toni kept in touch by email upon her return, giving me wonderful feedback. Her session had really made a difference to her. I decided to do something I wouldn't normally do and I shared the guidance story with her asking for her help.

At this stage in my growth I was also trying to teach myself to learn to receive; I had been told in meditation that I was out of balance as I was constantly giving to others and not receiving much in return. The more I continued to give, the more the universe would give me opportunities to keep on giving. So I decided I was going to learn to receive; a hard task. This was a first step of a new way of being for me.

Imagine my surprise and delight when Toni suggested I came over to Dubai! She went on to explain that she knew of a salon called Essentials and had spoken to the owner, Catherine, who would let me use her home where I could do my readings and healing sessions, and she also added that she would arrange clients. It all sounded too good to be true! I wondered if this was what it was like to be in flow with life. Had the guidance and inspiration come through because I allowed it to in meditation and silence?

The icing was on the cake when Mary's daughter Liz said I could stay at her apartment as they would be going on holiday for a few weeks. It all sounded so perfect, so orchestrated and we decided dates. All I had to do was inform Carl and book flights.

Then a very loud and clear message came through to me, that I had to take someone with me. That someone was Jayne; she had recently started learning Reiki master level, I had been teaching her for the last few months and she was showing signs of being a truly wonderful healer and communicator and a natural counsellor. I wasn't particularly surprised by the latest edition to this ever-growing jigsaw. The message then went on to say that Jayne had to be fast-tracked in her training. I wasn't told why! Just before booking the tickets, I called Jayne on her mobile – it went straight to voicemail so I left a message: 'Hi Jayne, it's Al here. I'm going to Dubai to do some work and was told that you need to come with me to take some light there. You are also to be fast-tracked. Call me back because I need your details to book the tickets.'

It must have sounded so casual. I always follow my guidance, so I must admit I do expect others to follow their's too, a bit presumptuous maybe. I can be a naughty angel too.

Shortly after, Jayne returned my call 'Aaaagh!' she screamed 'I'd love to.'

So that was how the trips to Dubai started.

We went for a week in May 2007, it was a huge success and we had a waiting list of people desperate to see us. What was so amazing and so confirming for me was that everyone kept thanking us for bringing the light to Dubai! The exact words that my angels and guides gave me in the original meditation! I was so overwhelmed with love and gratitude and thanked the angels for confirming this message. I was also grateful to myself for listening and following the messages I was given.

Jayne blossomed; we both did. Together we created something so beautiful and miraculous, everyone could see that we were genuine open-hearted healers and gifted teachers. They wanted to be in our energy.

The trip culminated with an Angel Day. An

Angel Day is a workshop or a joy shop, as I like to call them, whereby people who are interested in angels, or who simply feel they need to be there, turn up and we spend a day together – meditations and guidance. Jayne was there supporting me, or holding my energy as I often called it. We all gathered at Catherine's home and excitedly welcomed the angel attendees.

This time something was different. As usual I started the day with an opening meditation. Invoking the Archangels to come and join us – Archangel Michael, Archangel Raphael, Archangel Zadkiel and Archangel Chamuel, I became aware that my body and demeanour had started to change and take on energy. With each invocation I started to channel quite naturally through the spoken word; the Archangels were using my voice and my body to channel messages for the group. An hour and a half later the channelling ceased. Opening my eyes I could see the impact on the group, tears of happiness and joy filled the room.

The only way I can describe it is that it felt as if I'd left my physical body once again and I returned with a jump back into it as the last Archangel channelled.

Looking at a somewhat surprised Jayne she

returned my gaze by silently wording 'what the hell happened?' I shrugged my shoulders as if to say 'I don't know', trying to steady my unusually heavy body, I then surveyed the room once more. To my amazement and delight people were crying tears of joy and there was so much laughter. Now I knew why this happened to me; each person in that room had got something from one of those channelled messages. I've never seen or experienced anything like it, and I knew a gift had been awakened that day.

One of the beautiful souls there was a lady from Canada called Stella, she cried all day long and as she left exhausted but elated she told me that this day had changed her life. I welcomed her saying so, but didn't truly appreciate it until a year later when she invited me to stay at her family home in appreciation of this gift.

Later that evening, Jayne and I were enjoying a nice cold beer at the Birj Hotel looking out over the sea, and Jayne said to me, 'you just don't get it do you Ali?' 'Get what?' I said. 'You just don't get what you do to people.' And you know what? I didn't. That was to come much later.

The next day upon our return, Jayne and I sat in the airport lounge at Dubai airport reflecting back on the whole experience. We were absolutely exhausted, you could say running on empty, but no, we had so much energy, so much light and so much love within us and around us. We started to notice that as people went past us they would stop and stare, often turning back around to take another look. At first I asked Jayne if I had a bogey hanging from my nose, or was my skirt tucked into my knickers! 'What could they see?' we asked. Then a strong message was shouted at me, 'your light' was the answer, 'they can see your light shining so brightly. Well done. You have come far.' My angels were thanking us for our trip. They continued to pour their love into my heart. This time I was the one receiving their love and gratitude – bliss, pure bliss. After this message was given to me tears of pure joy and gratitude spilled down my face. 'Whatever is it?' Jayne enquired. 'I'm so happy Jayne, I just so love my job.' And then to top it all I heard the most beautiful angelic music being sung and played to me, into my ear that is non-hearing. I have often heard this music when something beautiful and empowering is due to happen. This time the angels were applauding Jayne and I for listening to this guidance, following our hearts, following the truth and in turn opening up people's hearts so they may go and do it to others.

This first trip left the unanswered question why did Jayne have to be fast-tracked? We weren't told why then, that would come later, much later.

So the light had been taken to Dubai, and my goodness it was needed. The people who live there constantly block out the light and glare from the desert sun. Driving round in great big 4x4s with blacked out windows, the air con on full at home and work. In the intense sun we often witnessed people run from their home into the car; the light doesn't stand a chance. Many of the ex-pats don't use the beach; 'it's for the tourists' they would say. They then book into the local salon for a fake tan.

That says it all about Dubai; fake, things not always what they seem on the surface, so many beautiful souls looking for the light, for something to fulfil them once and for all, many of them not even aware that's what they are doing.

So we returned home, exhausted but jubilant. Carl and my boys could see a change in me; they were more interested with what I'd bought them at Duty Free, but I'm sure they were pleased to have me home.

We were invited back in November, this time for two weeks. It was agreed that the original formula worked; I would do a reading for half an hour and then Jayne would do half hour slots of healing, so each person that came to us had the mutual benefit of having some healing and some guidance from their angels and their spiritual team. It worked so beautifully.

So the journey continued... Jayne and I went back to Dubai the following November. Another successful trip but it had a sour note to it. Toni who arranged the first trip also insisted on helping second time round; something didn't feel right and I wasn't looking forward to the trip. I couldn't put my finger on it and meditation didn't give me answers, maybe a lesson was due to be learnt.

The eve of our departure, Carl picked up on my nervousness and said 'it's not too late to cancel you know Al.' How could I cancel? I would be letting people down; we were fully booked for our healing and reading sessions. I had also decided to end the visit with an Angel Joy shop on the final day bringing the trip to a climax, and tickets had already been sold. I wasn't fully aware what was going on behind the scenes; with the beauty of hindsight I now recognise it as the first stage of giving my power away as I call it.

Pushing these nagging feelings away, I met Jayne at the airport ready for takeoff. We enjoyed the journey and the champagne; the drink of the angels we joked.

After arriving in the early hours, Brian, Toni's partner was waiting for us to take us to the accommodation. When we saw him I noticed the energy between us wasn't quite the same as last time; it had dropped. We all felt it, yet no words were said.

On the way to our accommodation, Brian told us that he and Toni had recently completed the same Angel Therapy course with Doreen as they were so inspired by my gift. A wonderful compliment; I didn't feel threatened by them being in competition with me, quite the opposite, it would mean they would carry on with the LIGHT work when we left.

The next day was a rest day where Jayne and I could acclimatise ourselves to the heat and recover from jetlag... and the champagne. We were due to start our busy schedule the following day and we knew there wouldn't be many chances to rest and sunbathe on this trip.

Brian had left us with a pay as you go mobile 'in case we needed anything'. This wasn't quite the true purpose behind it; Brian and Toni rang it constantly asking for guidance, as well as to bitch about fellow ex-pats. All very uncomfortable; this wasn't what the trip was about. We were determined not to join in with their dramas. Still feeling uneasy, Jayne screened the calls so I could rest, as interestingly vertigo was threatening to pounce once more. What was not in balance this time I pondered?

'What on earth is going on?' I asked. Again the answer wasn't forthcoming; or was I ignoring it?

After a fitful night's sleep where I dreamt about being attacked, Jayne and I set off to see Catherine, our salon-owner friend where we were based. What I didn't expect and what totally threw me off guard was seeing Toni awaiting our arrival armed with a long list of jobs she wanted us to carry out: hand out her and Brian's angel therapy business cards, their flyer for an angel day the week after ours, sell Toni's handmade jewellery, her mum's angel paintings... As the energy crashed, I was beginning to question the validity of this person. Had she looked after us so well on the first trip to lull us into a false sense of security, watch how we worked, then piggy-back off from our work? Pulling myself back from falling into drama once more, I corrected myself and said 'no, it's about bringing more love and light to Dubai, helping souls remember who they are and providing them with spiritual nourishment.'

The uneasiness grew as the reality became apparent. I simply wanted to do 'my thing' as I called it, as did Jayne, yet the alarm bells were ringing. So what did I do about it? Nothing! I pushed it aside and decided to get on with the task in hand. Was I still giving my power away?

After a shaky start the love soon started to flow and work its magic, Jayne's faith in me was inspiring and together we got into the zone and did our thing! We soon returned to the bliss state and forgot all about Toni's demands. We didn't sell anything; the goods seemed to disappear in the loving energy and no one enquired about them, so we didn't push it.

The story continued: we had an amazing two weeks, yet it was tainted by the 'angel couple's' demands, and we didn't leave as friends this time. Some good did come out of this trip though, we made friends with the salon's owner Catherine; a strong woman who against all the odds after being abandoned by her husband with two small girls had made a very successful business. She had observed how we worked and had passed the integrity test. Catherine told us that unfortunately, the actions we experienced were common in Dubai. Dog eat dog! If there was a way of making money, people would take advantage of it. Toni and Brian saw us as a means of carrying on with the angel work and used it to their advantage. How sad, yet I knew it was true.

All in all, there were four trips to Dubai. Jayne didn't return with me again – when we returned home she was diagnosed with breast cancer. Ironically Jayne and I had started up monthly breast cancer healing groups (to support and offer healing to anyone who was going through the experience of breast cancer) a year before; she was now one of those people who needed the healing and support.

Jayne's following year was taken up with a mastectomy, chemotherapy and radiotherapy. This is why Jayne was fast-tracked. Her experience in Dubai had not only strengthened her faith and belief, it had also shown her that she was not alone; surrounded by angels. Jayne plugged into this strength to get her through this gruelling task of survival. What a sight for sore eyes; her beautiful red hair disappeared, her smile broadened. Accompanying her to the specialist cancer wing at the hospital for chemo one time, the nurses didn't believe Jayne was a patient. She was clearly not a victim to this disease; dressed up in her best clothes and made up, we arrived in style in her new Saab soft top; a present to herself, Jayne was a lady who liked to arrive in style!

Once her treatment was over, Jayne holidayed in Mexico. A text summed up her gumption; 'I'm sitting near a nudist beach Ali; oh no I'll have to get my tit out!' Cancer no more – I'm delighted to say she beat it. Go girl!

The final trip

My final trip to Dubai was very challenging in many ways. I was going solo, long haul from Birmingham to Dubai. The nerves set in. In my heart of hearts I knew that this trip to Dubai was probably my final trip to share my gift. This trip was to spread some more light with people who too wanted to learn how to capture and hold that light and pass it onto others so they may become awakened. So it was decided that I would share the knowledge of Reiki and the tools of Angel Therapy and I had four eager souls waiting for me to spend the next five days bringing them up to Master teacher level so they could then pass on the tools and knowledge.

Awarded By Angels

This time I was invited to stay at Stella's villa; the Canadian lady who had been so moved on the Angel Joy shop. That day gave her the strength and energy to make some very determined changes. It was only on this trip that I was to realise the impact the Angel Day and the presence of my gift had upon Stella. When Stella had heard that I was making another trip to Dubai she insisted that I spent the ten days with her and her family. This very kind offer overwhelmed me; I was still learning the art of receiving and knew there was something new stirring, more lessons to be learnt, so I embraced the offer with the love it was given to me.

As with each visit to Dubai we were always shown a theme and I wondered what the theme would be this time. I really wanted to enjoy the whole experience of flying solo so arriving in good time, I asked the angels to look after me. I would have loved to have flown business class, but the funds weren't available so for this time at least I was seated in economy class. I was a bit cheeky and asked my angels to provide me with a window seat; imagine my surprise when I was told it was a full flight, but I was assigned a window seat as well as an empty seat next to me, the only empty seat on the flight. When

I arrived at the seat number on my boarding pass, there was a man sitting in my seat. 'Excuse me, you are sitting in my seat, would you mind moving?' A very confident air surrounded me resulting in this chap courteously yet with resistance doing as he was asked! 'Ooh the power,' giggling to myself as I sat down and perused the menu. This was going to be fun. I wondered if the theme was about women re-claiming their power.

After a great flight, I arrived at Dubai airport feeling very tired and just wanted to get to my hotel room. It's a huge airport and you can get lost really quickly and easily. So I knew that even though it was now about midnight, by the time I got to the villa it would be about two in the morning. Based on this I booked a hotel room just for the few hours so I could get my head down and then have a shower and arrive at Stella's house bright and early for a 10am start. This was the plan. I'm sure by now you realise that sometimes plans can go awry and this was one occasion when that happened. I had previously made the booking at my local travel agency to spend the night at a hotel in Dubai – £65 isn't a great amount of money in Dubai, but I thought it would get me a clean, comfortable room with the purpose that I could get a few hours sleep, have a shower and then leave to have breakfast with Stella before we started teaching and sharing the knowledge of Reiki. So you can imagine my surprise when the first taxi driver refused to take me to the hotel, it was now one thirty and I was feeling jet-lagged. I was hot and dusty and wanted to get into bed and have a few hours sleep.

It was quite unusual to have a taxi driver turn you down in Dubai, they are very much programmed to serve, so I must admit I started to feel a little bit aware that all was not well. I then found a taxi driver who said he would take me to the hotel. After driving around for at least an hour I thought we were lost. We weren't, we were exactly where we were meant to be. It was the part of Dubai you don't see in the glossy brochures; dirty, ugly and awful heavy, low energy, the driver insisted this was where I was staying. It was the area where the Indian workers imported to work on the new buildings lived. Not very plush at all, in fact it was very scary to witness. The taxi driver announced that he was leaving me right in the middle of the street; he said he would leave me here and I would have to walk to the hotel. I knew that I was possibly at risk, and as I surveyed my new environment it was quite clear that I was indeed at risk. Exiting the taxi I saw many men pouring onto the streets, some drunk, some smoking some dodgy cigarettes and they were calling out at me and pulling at my clothes as I walked by. I immediately returned to victimhood. I also quickly became aware that I had to dig deep within and link into the tools that had saved my life up to this moment. So I called upon God and the angels to help me, in complete and utter faith that my pleas would be heard and answered.

Just at that moment I felt a beautiful warm energy surrounding and encompassing me and my stature became stronger, taller and with more presence; not bad for a five foot three shorty! I then instructed the taxi driver that he was indeed taking me directly to the hotel, and if he did not respond to my request then he would not get paid and furthermore I would call a policeman, who would not take kindly to him leaving a British woman alone in the streets of Dubai. That's all it needed. He quickly walked with my case to the hotel.

It was an extremely dark and suspect-looking hotel that was to be my home for the next six hours. The taxi driver left rather quickly and I realised he truly did not want to be in this hotel. Did it hide secrets? I pondered.

The two male receptionists took my name and continued to ask questions: 'Are you here to work, Mrs Ward?' I hadn't got a licence to work in Dubai; I was told I wouldn't need one; if I was asked just to say I was staying with friends. 'No, I'm here to visit friends.' Which was sort of true. They continued to ask me the same questions. 'Are you sure you're not here to work, Mrs Ward?' 'No. I'm just here for a few hours and then I'm going to get a taxi and go and spend some time with my friend at her villa. I've only come to this hotel because of the arrival time. Now please will you take me to my room?' The smaller of the two men then escorted me to my room. The journey from reception to the room that would be my home for the next few hours was short; I heard some quite disturbing and alarming noises; women screaming, a child crying. At first I thought it was the norm, you often hear children crying in the middle of the night, babies crying out for their mother. This felt different though. I was feeling more and more alarmed, sensitive to the growing energies and fear really was beginning to set in. Upon arriving at my room the male receptionist said in broken English, 'here, leave keys outside door.' I looked at him confused, questioning him in disbelief 'sorry?' 'Here' he repeated 'key on outside of door.' I looked at him straight in the eye and firmly said 'no, here leave key inside door.' We continued this volleying debate for a couple of minutes, when I realised I'd had enough, then I said firmly with all my might 'here I leave keys inside door,' and with that I firmly pushed him away, closed the door and locked it. Phew, what a relief.

As I looked around the small room it wasn't quite what I'd imagined for my money's worth. The bed was a small double bed, had holes in the sheets and in the centre of the bed it had a small tea towel. So I walked into the bathroom and thought maybe a quick shower might take away the energy of what I had just experienced, but there weren't any towels, just small hand towels. I hadn't brought any towels with me because I was staying at my friend's villa and didn't think it was necessary. The room didn't feel quite as clean as I would have liked and even though it was incredibly hot and humid, I decided to lie fully clothed on the bed to get a couple of hours sleep. That was very optimistic; I don't think I slept at all for those few hours I was in that room. The constant stream of people walking past the door, and continual crying of women and babies was extremely disturbing. I was by this time becoming more fearful and anxious, but still I couldn't phone and ask for help. It was now well into the early hours. I pulled myself together, reminded myself that I was safe and protected and once more tried to sleep, aware that in a few hours I would be teaching and sharing in the knowledge of Reiki so I knew I had to have my energy 100% to deliver that.

Eventually the first light of the sun in Dubai started to rise with the sounds of calling for prayers – thank goodness, some sort of normality. I also found the calling for prayers very reassuring, and I decided then even though it was about six thirty I was going to leave the hotel. It's amazing isn't it how when the sun comes up everything seems that little bit more bearable? I was still feeling fearful, but I knew I had to push those fears away and stay confident, so I showered and blotted myself dry with the small hand towels, quickly packed my case and left the building at speed. The two men were still at reception, they looked in my direction as I left without a word.

Landing outside in the bustling Dubai street the sharp heat tore right through my clothes, already the traffic was at full pelt. Where on earth could I get a taxi from? I went back into reception and asked them for a taxi. They just looked blankly at me. They didn't want to know, they didn't want to help, so I left them. I decided to walk towards the main bustle of the three highways and hail down a taxi, but it wasn't happening. So what do you do when you're stuck in a foreign place without anyone around who knows you?

I asked for help! I stood there, coat in one hand, bag on the other shoulder, feeling extremely weary and quite frankly pissed off, but then calmness came over me as I linked in and asked for help. 'Please someone help me get to Stella's so I can do what I came here to do.' Literally as I finished my request for help, a taxi driver with a fare already in his taxi arrived at the side of the road. 'Quickly get in, I will take you. You will not get a taxi here. Here is not safe.' And with that he bundled my case into the boot and I quickly jumped into the back of the car. 'Thank you' and I looked this beautiful man straight in the eyes and said 'do you know you're an angel?' His face beamed with light and gratitude and he said 'me?' questioningly. 'You are my angel,' I said 'thank you so much for stopping.' 'You're not safe here, Miss' he said. He noted Stella's address and within minutes I arrived at the huge gates to her villa. What a difference a short drive can make; from a small shabby hotel room to grand gates gently opening. Revealing a beautiful building, a swimming pool and grounds to match, I was in a very different place. I counted four cars! I knew Stella was living on her own with two of her children so why did they need four cars I asked. Hey, that's Dubai!

I was duly welcomed into Stella's villa and proceeded to tell her about the night before. 'You didn't go there?' she exclaimed when I told her the name of the hotel. 'I did, I booked it at my local village travel agents. I cannot believe they sent me there.' 'Did you know that was a brothel?' Stella asked; my thoughts had been confirmed. The first and last time that Alison Ward was to stay in a brothel!

After several mugs of coffee and warm homemade pancakes I deposited my case in the guest room; a huge contrast to the hotel room earlier. I then prepared for the arrival of the other students to come and start their Reiki journey.

We had a wonderful five days together, sharing in the knowledge and practice of Reiki and Angel Therapy; much laughter and love resumed. All the students were women and all identified with the new theme of the trip; women giving their power away. We used the example of the brothel to discuss what drove women to prostitution, particularly in a Muslim country with all the risks involved.

Then later in the week, whilst delivering soul guidance sessions, I met a huge amount of women from all walks of life who continued to give their power away; often to men. This reminded me of how I gave my power away to Junior's father, Bob. Many of these men were wealthy, unfortunately the wealth added to the disempowerment of these women living in Dubai. They had to have permission to work, permission to have a bank account and without their husbands say so they were not allowed either of these things. Dubai is a land of power and prosperity and is definitely ego filled. Alongside its beauty and richness lie a lot of lost souls, a lot of people there striving for success.

Success, what is success? I asked; to many it is about having money and all the things that go with money: the beautiful homes, the lifestyle, the cars, the drivers, the maids. But unfortunately some of the men in Dubai felt that wealth and status gave them licence to treat their women poorly, often embarking on extra-marital affairs to the obvious detriment of their marriages. So many of the women I saw that week were in relationships where they knew their partners were having affairs with many women, but they were also trapped by their lifestyle that had become a necessity. They relied upon the money, the lifestyle and everything that came with it. The networking, the beautiful clothes, the parties - part of that they enjoyed, but it also entrapped them.

Not all the women I met that week were unhappy, not at all, a lot of them came to see me because they were finding themselves and trying to look for a purpose, and some came out of curiosity. I met a real mix of women on that last journey; I hope that their sessions gave them some peace and hope, giving them permission to regain their power.

(When I returned home from that final trip I wrote a letter to the travel agents and followed it up with a phone call, but they were in complete denial, there are no such things as brothels in Dubai, they exclaimed. If only they knew.)

So as the trip came to an end, the final day gave me the opportunity to reflect; a wonderful day was spent with the newly qualified Reiki masters. It started off in a Yoga class; I couldn't believe how my body moved into shapes. I noticed how confident and how in his gift the Yogi was giving me confidence, thus my body moved into positions I didn't know it could. Although extremely tired, I gained energy from the Yoga session. It filled me with light and energy; after two hours, we then had a beautiful lunch and went shopping. I was then driven to the local angel salon as I nick-named Catherine's salon, Essentials, from where Jayne and I had previously enjoyed beauty treatments following our weeks' work at Catherine's home.

Upon returning to the villa, Stella and I spent the early part of the evening in the balmy heat on Stella's porch talking about the week and the discoveries we had made. It was then that the realisation hit me that the gift I had been given had started to develop further. I also realised that it had helped many people.

Stella then informed me how the Angel Day the previous year had changed her life. It had filled her with confidence and faith, and knowledge that she would be alright, and that she was indeed okay, that she was being provided for and that would continue. She went home and informed her husband she wanted to separate. Her strength, her faith and her determination to become further enlightened gave her the power to formalise a new life for her and her family. Now sitting on her porch, she was now happily divorced, living in a beautiful villa. Her wealth had given her the possibilities to work with other spiritual teachers and this in turn had started to bring forward her gift. She shared with me what it had meant to her and how much the impact of not only my gift, but my presence had upon her. At first I was a bit embarrassed and in denial to accept such a compliment, but something was telling me to truly listen this time, and to accept what she was giving me, she was giving me the gift of gratitude and I could not deny this gift. Finally it occurred to me that I had to fully accept the gift that I had, that by being in denial of this gift, or hiding from this gift, reduced its strength. It was then I heard someone shouting in my head; 'now will you accept your gift?'

Yes, I accepted. I shared this announcement with Stella; we both chinked our glasses of wine and said cheers. Thank you Stella for giving me your insight and showing me your gratitude, I now accept my gift.

"Angel" Alison Ward

LESSONS LEARNT

- *Learn to give back to the community; it gives you so much satisfaction and joy in return as well as helping others.*

- *Be aware people are people; do not expect everyone to be like you with the same morals and truth.*

- *Look at inspiring quotes and writing to buoy your faith.*

- *Believe in you and your gifts; they have been given to you to nurture and develop them as you would a child.*

- *Listen to your guidance, learn the art of meditation.*

- *A simple way to start is by sitting comfortably with your back straight and your palms on your lap. Breathe in through your nose and hold for two counts, exhale deeply, letting go.*

- *Repeat this until you are at one with your breath.*

- *If your mind starts to wander, bring your focus back to your breath. Practice the same time every day; morning is ideal.*

Inspirations, Coincidences And Teaching The Police

Now in ownership and acceptance of my gift, the business developed. I was shown many situations that further confirmed the importance of recognising coincidences and synchronicities as confirmation of being on the right path.

There have been so many; I can't remember them all. One recent example was when I was looking for a new treatment room to work from; I had been working from home for years, but in 2008/2009 the plot of land adjacent to our house had planning permission for four houses. The noise and dust meant that it was no longer a quiet sanctuary for people to come to so

I asked the angels for help. 'Please tell me where my new treatment room is based?'

As usual it wasn't too long before the answer came. Remember, by now I diligently practised receiving my guidance on a daily basis by being still and silent, breathing in, holding for two then exhaling. This simple practice gave the guidance, inspiration, imagination, chance to come through.

I had just spent a fun-filled day with a like-minded soul in Shrewsbury; shopping, lunch and a bit more shopping. As my friend dropped me off at the station I exclaimed; 'I wish my angels would show me where to work from.'

Just then my mobile rang; it was Dad informing me he had just had a haircut at Wards in the village – my namesake. Slightly confused as to why Dad was telling me the minutiae of his life he proceeded to tell me that there was a large treatment room at the back. Not only that, it was available for let. How wonderful, the angels had got me a place to work from in my area with my name on the sign; bliss. I met Sharon, the owner, later that evening and we hit it off immediately. I was to work from there for a whole year until able to work back at my sanctuary.

The phrase 'what goes around, comes around' is

a familiar saying that we often express at times of strife. The next true story talks about me teaching the police.

In the spring and early summer of 2009 a friend of mine whose job was involved in teaching police recruits in the first eighteen weeks of their training, approached me and asked me if I would consider giving a talk about the attack or, as I now like to call it, The Awakening, and how as a victim and those around me were affected. I asked the family to see if they were happy with me doing this, and they all agreed that as long as I was okay with it then to go ahead.

A couple of weeks later I turned up at a Police Training Centre in the West Midlands, where there were eighteen recruits in the sixth week of their eighteen-week training course. (Coincidently we live at number 18).

I was greeted by my friend Jenny and her sergeant and asked if I was prepared before I went into the room. They asked me if I would 'sock it to them', to involve them so they could really appreciate and be a part of my experience enabling them to view it with more knowledgeable eyes and ears. I decided for one time only that I would allow myself to go back to that raw place of memory and share with them the entire happenings of 5th July 1994 when my day and my life changed forever.

I spent an hour and a quarter with those recruits and what was absolutely wonderful to see was that many of them were sitting on the edge of their chairs as I shared with them my torturous moments on that fateful day. I allowed myself to fully experience the pain once more and I felt it. I may have thought it lay dormant within me, but as soon as I opened the door the dormancy leapt into life. I touched the rawness of the pure pain, not only the physical pain but the emotional pain of how one human being could do this to another, including their own son. I told them about the anxious moments as I waited to discover whether Junior was alive or dead. I told them about the help of my neighbours and the local community and the sloppy behaviour of the police and their attitude towards me as a single mother. What I tried to convey and tried to educate these new recruits in, is that you should never judge another, particularly in such events as those we experienced on that day.

I recounted the time two days after The Awakening when a photo still hadn't been taken of my injuries. Eventually two police officers came to my parents' home, where I was now living and said they needed to take some photos. The human body is quite amazing in many ways; it was incredible how my injuries had started to heal up, my physical injuries. As a consequence, I didn't look half as bruised and battered as I had done a couple of days earlier much to my annoyance. I know this might sound odd, but I needed them to see the evidence of what this person did to me, if they didn't see it with their own eyes then they wouldn't believe it.

I told the recruits now I was truly in victimhood; when one is a victim, a victim of this so called 'domestic violence', there is such shame and embarrassment, a feeling of being weak and pitiful, and there is also a strange protective feeling you have towards your attacker, as absurd as that may sound, it is the truth. This was evident when I gave my statement to the police, my sister Louise sitting by my side evidently shocked by my protectiveness towards this person. The only thing that I can say upon reflection is that there was still some loyalty, yes this man committed this offence, but he was still the natural father of my son. I don't have that loyalty today, there is no emotion held for that man.

I felt shocked, appalled and victimised once more

when these police officers started to make fun of the size of the breasts that had saved my life, and meant the knife kept hitting against bone. They had dismissed all ounce of compassion, to them it was a laugh and I was once more helpless; a victim with no voice, words unspoken. When one of them asked me to turn around so they could take photos of my back I refused and put my clothes back on; without pushing me they left, job done.

Once more I slipped into a victim. I had begun to feel that maybe it was my fault; maybe there was something in me that created this attitude, this behaviour from men. I had been brought up to respect police officers, to respect the law and here were two police officers laughing and goading me. Shameless, is all I can say.

As the story continued, the new recruits were gripped. I continued to sock it to them, giving them the full truth and consequential impact. I told them about when Bob was on bail his probation officer phoned me to say that 'Bob is doing well, he's going to the gym, he's getting fit.' No thought for my feelings; the friendliness, the over-friendliness of the probation officer and the lack of communication to me again was a huge oversight and a huge injustice.

I wasn't even informed that Bob broke his bail conditions and was back in my hometown until two days afterwards. I found out through the grapevine, his gossiping friends eager to be the first to inform me, witnessing yet more pain from his victim.

I'm sure there were many more occasions where my family and I were let down by the police and so called supporting services. The one thing that hurt me considerably more was the newspaper article that stated I had superficial injuries. When the doctor put a ruler through the wound to measure the depth of penetration, again I felt violated but of course they were doing their job, this time with love and concern.

How can you call that a superficial injury? My leg that I brought up as protection for my chest had suffered a very deep wound that just missed a main artery, my whole leg was bruised and bloody for two weeks and I had to walk with sticks. How is that a superficial injury? I had lost my hearing, again is that a superficial injury?

Years later, the criminal injury compensation board awarded me just under £11,000 for the events that happened that day. They wouldn't accept my lack of hearing following the attack as there was some conflict about whether the attack caused that, which I had to accept.

After appealing, I was called back to stand before the awarding Judge. I asked why I hadn't been reimbursed for the deposit I lost on my rented house due to the blood stains on the carpet and walls. The landlord quite rightly had to have them replaced.

On answering my question, the judge said 'Mrs Ward I am not here to pay your cleaning bills.'

To which I replied; 'I am so sorry my lord to have bled all over the carpet M'lord.'

All these events and experiences had created an angry person. I had felt let down, unsupported. I felt that the judicial system had hugely let my family and I down. My life meant nothing to them, nor did my son's.

Bearing all this in mind, on this day faced with new police recruits, I took the opportunity to invite them along with me on this reflective journey, back to that fateful day. They walked alongside me and they were duly shocked and appalled. I was so grateful that they heard my story, that they acknowledged my story and believed my story. I didn't make it up, it was real and they believed me.

At the end of the session that had lasted an hour

and a quarter, I was taken to a room to have some light refreshments. Looking concerned Jen asked me how I was. 'Numb,' was my answer. Not many words passed after that and for the few days that followed this numbness stayed with me. I was very quiet and very introverted. I believe that was me just putting it back to bed, back in that closet where it lurked for many years and that is where it now stays.

The reason I am sharing this with you is that I wish you to hear my story and to reassure you that if you are in a difficult relationship, in an abusive relationship, or going through a trauma, a place of despair where there is no hope maybe this book will give you hope, will give you strength. You have the strength to change, you have that strength within you, just please find it – it is there.

Later on that evening when I was sitting quietly at home with a large glass of wine, I had a text from Jen saying, 'congratulations, today you have changed the police force.' Whether that was true or not doesn't really matter to me. What mattered more than anything was that these new recruits had heard and believed me; my story had made a difference. They were going out into the world as police officers, with maybe some more knowledge, compassion and understanding. Maybe they will think before jumping into a situation and hopefully they will see that the people involved in any sort of situation are real people with real lives who experience pain. As long as it changed one person's view on that day, then I'm happy.

LESSONS LEARNT

- *Watch out for coincidences and synchronicity; they are life's way of letting you know you're on the right track.*

- *Sometimes going over the past is an opportunity to further heal from it; if you find you're repeatedly going backwards, seek professional help.*

- *Resistance is often an opportunity for growth; I didn't want to share my story with the police, yet I knew it had to be told for their awareness.*

- *There are many coincidences within this book; learn to recognise and appreciate them in your life and they will grow in regularity; I'm a great believer in that the more you trust, the more you'll be given in return.*

"Angel" Alison Ward

Crisis Of Faith

Thirteen years after I started doing this work professionally and sharing my gift I started to realise the weariness within me was growing, and upon reflection I realised that I hadn't had much time off. The LIGHT work had been constant. When I first started my youngest son, David, was 2 years old and not sleeping through the night, I had a full time job at the Hospice, a husband, a post-traumatic son who needed help, continual help, and a home as well as our lovely dog, Basil. On top of this, continuing to work and build up a business had taken its toll upon me and the family. Up until this point in 2009, I worked at speed, I couldn't turn my back on the continual, ever-growing guidance I was given, it was beyond my freewill. But now in October 2009, I kept experiencing huge overwhelming bouts of extreme tiredness, even exhaustion.

Once more I sat and asked for guidance. The message I was given was clear; 'take three months off, recoup your energy, stop teaching Reiki and pass the clinics on – it is time to release yourself from others and finish this book.' I was somewhat bewildered because I also interpreted that I was meant to stop teaching and practising Reiki, and yet that had been my passion for so many years. In conflict to that feeling, I also knew on a deeper level that this was truth. I relayed this message to Carl, who confirmed that indeed I looked weary and it was time to take some time off to rest and continue the journey of this book. This coincided with three months that were Carl's busiest time of the year, and we worked out that we could manage financially, just about, with only Carl's wage coming in.

The next step was to announce this semi-retirement to the group of people who had helped me run the clinic. If you remember I had started the healing clinics back in 1998 at the Hospice and had continued them on and off over the years. There were now several clinics a month all run by volunteer healers. The idea of the clinics was to give back to the community, whilst sharing in the love of Reiki and what it provides to us all. Many people within the local community had benefitted from receiving regular healing for all sorts of problems – physical, mental and emotional – with great success. Any donations received covered costs allowing the clinics to grow and develop. It was also an opportunity for newly qualified Practitioners to practise their new skill with the support of experienced healers and teachers; a 'win/win' situation for all.

A meeting was organised to share the guidance with two of the four master teachers one day after Saturday clinic. Coincidentally it happened that I was no longer able to help out on a Saturday, as David had been accepted into a new football team and his training happened to be every Saturday, 10am to midday. Carl worked every Saturday so it was down to me to take David to and from training. The clinic work had to go. Ironically the practicality of everyday life stepped in to help me accept and make the decision to leave and take the guidance further.

So after clinic that day I explained to Carl that I was off to the pre-arranged meeting to share my decision to take some time out and complete this book. Imagine my surprise when the reaction I received from these two spiritual teachers was challenging, questioning and not at all in keeping with Reiki trained and Reiki practised people. One of them announced that she was disappointed with my decision and with me as their teacher. The two combined their energies and worked against me and my guidance for a further hour. What they had done? They had taken my decision and made it about them.

Bewildered, surprised and shocked I continued to state that if I did not honour this guidance I wouldn't be true to myself; life had taught me to listen to this inner knowledge and to act upon it, I wasn't going to turn my back on it now because they were disappointed in me. All too often in the past, I hadn't listened and acted upon my guidance and look where that got me.

The decision I had made was given to me, it wasn't an ego-based decision, I knew that; if anything it had taken me by surprise. I live my life following guidance; I know truth when I hear it and this was truth.

You can imagine that their response was extremely alarming, surprising and incredibly hurtful. One and a half hour's later I returned home. I chose not to share this experience with Carl straight away, as the following day I was due to fly out to Spain to spend a week with Carl's parents. They had retired there six years previously and Beryl, Carl's mum had not been well. Carl wasn't able to go due to his workload, so he asked if I would go and spend some time with his parents and help them if needed. I decided that the week away would be a valuable time for reflection, not only on the last few years, but the whole journey since The Awakening in 1994. I knew that there was a new direction coming for me, but I didn't know what.

After a fitful night's sleep I woke up early in the morning to arrive at the airport for this long awaited week of rest and recuperation. I'm happy so say it delivered exactly that; the lifestyle my in-laws have in Spain is very slow, laid-back, relaxing and fun. The days would often be spent getting up in our own time, having a long breakfast and then taking a ride out somewhere, having a coffee, meeting friends, having lunch. It was beautiful, absolutely beautiful. This slower pace of life gave me more time to reflect and consider the guidance and recent events. I began to share my experiences with Sid, my father-in-law, and thankfully he reassured me that he thought I had worked very hard for a long time, and that maybe it was time for me to withdraw for a few months and see what that new energy would bring. That awareness and acknowledgement was just what I needed. I also recognised that the space gave me more ammunition for resting and taking a back seat. I had also notice the Reiki energy change over the last year; people were beginning to disrespect it and dishonour it including the two teachers whose reaction was so bizarre. I remembered showing them how to practise the ancient ceremony of passing Reiki attunements. The Buddhist monks used to practise this ceremony to bring the healing energy into their students. I was always shown respect and honour whilst illustrating this to previous Reiki Masters but these two fooled around during the presentation in total disrespect. I did share my disappointment with them and explained I had never witnessed it before that day. Other situations also came forward in my memory; giving me more comfort in my decision.

Upon my return I shared my experiences with Carl; he was particularly disappointed with one of the ladies as we thought she was a friend. We offered her a place to stay following her five-month visit to India. She accepted our offer and lived with for five weeks. She had witnessed firsthand how full our lives were with my work, the constant phone calls, emails, calls for help, so her reaction was incredibly startling to both of us, even after a week of rest and reflection.

Carl expressed that maybe they were more reliant upon me than they had realised and that me withdrawing my energy from them was like a rug being pulled from beneath them. That in turn caused me distress as I am a great believer in empowering people and giving them the tools to become empowered. Clearly things had to change.

One of the master teachers I hadn't shared this information with in its fullness, was a beautiful soul called Sarah. So after sharing with Carl first, I then contacted Sarah informing her of everything that had happened. I love the name Sarah; my angel's name, interestingly all the Sarahs I've met since are all so lovely too. Refreshingly, Sarah welcomed my guidance and my decision with a huge open heart and a wonderful warm hug. 'I will support you whatever, Alison. If that's your guidance then you must follow it.' This was true spirit and confirmation that when one recognises truth in another, support is offered. Relieved and grateful I shared with her the feelings of sadness and pain that had accompanied the decision and the reaction I had from the other two master teachers.

Sarah was not happy with this news and wanted to find out the reasons for their reaction for herself; suggesting we held another meeting with myself, Sarah and the two teachers to see if we could sort this out. The date and time was set for the following Thursday evening. I did feel anxious I must admit; there was also a great feeling of trepidation. But I knew it was part of the journey and part of the letting-go process. Arriving five minutes early at the venue, the two teachers were already there and Sarah was sitting slightly to the left. Straight away the energy felt very hard, judgemental and unpleasant as well as unwelcoming. As Sarah greeted me with a hug, we all then sat down and commenced small talk. After a few minutes, I brought the conversation around to the purpose of the meeting and I explained to the two master teachers that I was disappointed about their reaction and that I had felt interrogated by their questioning. Unfortunately, this was not what they felt they had experienced and the meeting resulted in us parting company. They also announced that they both had decided that they would be leaving the clinics and would not be helping any further.

This was an unexpected and sad decision.

Upon returning home, Carl had been waiting up for me as he knew it was probably going to be an uncomfortable meeting, and he could tell by my demeanour that it hadn't been a pleasant situation. I reassured him that I was okay and I would tell him more the following evening and insisted that he went to bed. He looked exhausted, the fourteen-hour days were taking their toll I noticed. He needed his rest. Just before retiring to bed that evening the phone rang; it was Sarah, the loving soul that had given me encouragement earlier in the meeting. Shaken by their reaction, she again pledged her support. She was surprised that people who had been trained would react in such a way. She further assured me that the decision I had made to take time out was indeed the right decision. It's quite strange, on one level I knew why they had reacted like that, but on a personal level I was so disappointed and so hurt. Over the coming days whenever I felt that hurt energy hit me I would rise above it and see that they really were working from ego and not from love. By now I've been in this trusting energy for so many years I have learnt to accept that when guidance is given in purity then it is indeed the truth, and if I endeavour to continue to work in truth and with light I must accept that some of the decisions that are given to me. I must also accept that some people do not like those decisions.

The saying – 'You can't please everybody all of the time' kept me going and a few months later as I'm writing this final chapter, there is a huge sense of relief that I listened to the guidance meant for me and my growth, and that I gave myself this time, this love and the acceptance of having a well-earned break. I'm now grateful that I released these two souls as they have to continue on with their journey and I am obviously no longer a part of it.

True friends

The day following the final meeting was a Friday, I was due to meet up with two very good friends of mine I met whilst working at the Hospice; Karen, who is one of my dearest friends, and the other is a lady called Irene who has been a hospice nurse for over twenty years and was in her retirement year, aged fifty five.

The last time I had seen Irene was in May when she came along to visit the healing clinics that were being run in my area. I had set these particular clinics up about two years earlier so all the Reiki trained people could give back to the community and keep their skills updated. It was often called my Vision as I had started them back in 1998 at the Hospice. I shared the vision with Irene; the Reiki clinics were to make it accessible to all, irrespective of gender, belief, race, or financial power. Naturally I observed that many of the volunteers initially felt this service was meant for the people who had limited finances, when in fact that was not the idea behind the Vision – making Reiki accessible to all, one might be financial wealthy, but spiritually poor. The idea of these clinics was so that people who wouldn't normally be open to receiving the beautiful energy of Reiki would come into the clinics and receive the healing power that it gives so their lives may become more balanced and in flow.

On that clinic day back in May 2010, Irene had witnessed the beauty of the clinics first hand. Irene was also a Reiki master, a skill she learnt in her nursing years. When she left the clinic that day she was full of the energy, full of love and delight; 'look at what you have achieved, Alison. There is no ego here, only love, I'm so proud of you.' Tears of joy ran down her face and we hugged.

Now five months later I was due to see Irene, the day after the horrible meeting but reticence was stopping me. On the day that Irene experienced the clinic, upon returning home she fell down the stairs and broke her neck. I felt responsible for the accident; I was to blame; surely if she hadn't visited the clinic that day she wouldn't have had that accident. Totally untrue, I know, but that's sometimes how I slip back into victimhood.

I began to realise that my sabotaging behaviour was trying to prevent me from seeing my true friends who genuinely love and care for me. This is often how the ego presents itself; trying to keep you separate from LOVE.

Ego is often referred to as the darker side of self. I don't quite like that term 'darker side'. I believe it to be a crucial part of us as human beings. To hide away from our shadow or dark self we are hiding away a part of us. By learning so much about me, the recovery and the tools found over the last sixteen years, I was not prepared to hide any aspect of who I am. So pushing through this resistance and the untruth about me being responsible I drove towards Irene's flat.

My ego has often jumped in whilst writing this book; 'who wants to read your book?' has often come up, as well as 'who do you think you are?' Often the ego will bring up lower patterns of thoughts and behaviour to prevent you from being fulfilled. I had learnt to recognise the signs so my journey to my true friends continued.

Leaving home later than planned the realisation of ego had delayed me; another sign of ego in play. I then put some washing in, and on the way I stopped to get some flowers. I then decided to give myself a bit of a shake, 'come on Alison, what do you think you're doing? You know you'll feel better when you see them.' Part of me did not want to see them that day because I was going to have to put on a false act. I was upset and feeling fragile from the night before at the meeting of the Master Teachers and didn't want my friends to see me in pain. I also recognised this protective pattern; I used to do it when I was still post-trauma, falsely believing that if I appeared ok, then all my loved ones would be ok. Of course this did not work so as this awareness started to grow within me, I decided once more the best form of revenge was happiness, openness and acceptance. So I turned the radio up full blast, sang at the top of my voice and drove to Irene's.

My mood now lifted, God I have an awful singing voice; it did make me laugh though as fellow motorists were forced to hear me sing!

I couldn't remember the road that Irene lived in although I had been there many times previously so I decided to ask for help. There it appeared in front of me. I couldn't remember the number of her flat, but funny enough my car was parked exactly outside her flat and I remembered it! That on its own, that remembrance is a miracle. My memory is shocking since the head injury of 1994.

As Irene welcomed me in, I could see that she looked incredibly well, a little bit stiff in movement, but hey wouldn't you expect that after a broken neck. As we walked up the stairs; the stairs that had committed that neck-breaking act five months earlier, I could smell the overwhelming odour of cleaning fluids and bleach. 'Blimey Irene, you've been going a bit crazy on the old bleach haven't you?' 'Tell me about it Al, I've been cleaning for the last two days ready for your visit.' With that I roared with laughter, anyone who knows me knows to take me as you find me, and I would do the same.

Walking into her kitchen armed with two

bunches of flowers; I was greeted by Karen's warm smiley face. Here we hugged and embraced and then I received another angelic hug from Irene, and instantly I felt at ease and in peace.

I then decided I needed to start our meeting with honesty and openness. 'Irene I'm really sorry what happened to you. I haven't been in contact with you because I actually thought it was my fault and I felt responsibility for you falling and breaking your neck after visiting me at the clinic. I know it's ridiculous but that's how I felt.' Pouring it all out, a huge sense of relief engulfed me.

'Alison there are a few things I need to tell you first' Irene said. Here we were stood in her small, gleaming kitchen yet there was a lovely large lounge waiting for us. 'Are we not going in the lounge?' I enquired. 'No, not just yet.' Irene insisted. 'I need to talk to you first.'

'Alison, there is someone who is having a crisis of faith and we need to help them. I have been given channelling for the last few days and I've been surrounded by angels and ascended masters who have given me instructions.' 'Oh, ok' I said, wondering who this person could be. Interestingly the three of us, including our friend V, who had passed on in May would occasionally get together and if we felt we needed to do some energy work for someone in need, or a far away country in crisis, we would join our energies as one and we would send out loving healing energy to the person or the situation. So I just presumed that is what we would be doing, that we would be linking our energy in, albeit without V, and we would be sending love and healing and acceptance to this person who was experiencing a crisis of faith. Now I don't know if you, the reader has realised that by now, since working with this loving accepting and Reiki energy all these years, if someone is in need you put all of your own needs to one side, instantaneously. So as soon as Irene informed us that someone was having a crisis of faith, all my feelings of emotional pain and upset were pushed aside and seemed so irrelevant knowing that someone else was in need. 'Ok then, who is it?' I enquired. 'Alison, darling, it's you.' Irene said. 'You are the one with the crisis of faith.'

Tears of gratitude or release, I'm not sure which, rolled down my cheeks. Irene then proceeded to tell me that she had created a beautiful energetic circle of truth in her living room, hence all the clearing and the cleaning. As Karen, Irene and I walked into the living room we naturally sat down and created a triangle. 'What's going on Irene?' I said.

'Alison, I need to tell you something and you need to listen. I've been surrounded the last two or three days by a great deal of spirits, by many angels and ascended masters and they have told me that you are having a crisis of faith. That two people have let you down very badly, very recently.' 'Fucking hell, Irene!' I exclaimed. 'You're good. That only happened last night.' She continued, 'They told me that you have been let down by two people. They have also told me that you are revered, that you have helped thousands of people.' 'Thousands?' I interrupted, questioningly. 'Yes, thousands of people over the years, and it is now time for you to take two or three months off, to rest, recoup, pass on the clinics, stop teaching Reiki and to write this book because it is going to be published.' My God, Irene was telling me the exact same guidance I had previously been given on many occasions word for word, and yet we hadn't spoken since May, and it was now October! When I'm alarmed I often resort to using swear words, I don't mean to offend you; and so it continued. 'Fucking hell Irene, you're good. I can't believe that.' And with that I continued to swear in exclamation. Laughter ripped around the room.

I then shared with my two true friends the recent experiences and the recent rejection of my decision. Upon doing so a great weight lifted from my shoulders and I knew that it was right, that what Irene had given me that day had been absolute confirmation of my truth; it was time to move on. It was time to take a new path and the only way this new path could start was to take some time out, to complete this book, completing the journey to full circle.

Irene then proceeded to tell me that on that day in May, when she visited the clinics, she came home and was full of the beautiful loving energy that had been created there. She then continued to share with us the story of how she fell down the stairs and broke her neck. In fact she said, she believed she had broken a contract made with God. She had told God that she would retire at fifty five, but when her birthday arrived, Irene became fearful of not having enough money, of not being provided for, so resorted to her old pattern as many of us do of ignoring the strong feeling that we must do something. Pushing that aside she decided she would stay on at the

Hospice, would continue to work, would continue to earn money and would possibly retire one, two, three, five years later.

'I had promised God that I would retire at fifty five' Irene said. 'I was pushed down the stairs to bring me back to my truth.' With this realisation Irene forgave herself and her old patterns.

What a powerful way to wake up to your truth. She then proceeded to say that while she was on the hospital bed in agony, she begged God to take her away due to the pain; as she was begging God a face appeared in front of her. It was my face. 'I saw your face, Al, and I saw that absolute trust that you knew you would always be provided for. I saw the love that was created in that clinic and I knew I would be okay. You saved my life.'

Of course you can imagine I couldn't accept that, lovely as it was. Irene and Karen gave me the wonderful gift of true friendship, trust and acceptance on that day. Through Irene's gift of channelling, she gave me confirmation of my guidance word for word as well as immense gratitude and acknowledgement that I had indeed helped many people and that now it was time to look after myself. Karen as always was sitting there sending out her love, her acceptance and her pride.

Karen is a woman that doesn't use many words, and was aware her presence was what was needed. She is a very powerful strong, loving person and her smile said it all. 'I think you're both amazing' she said. 'We're all amazing' was my answer and with that we hugged and continued to laugh, and then ate pizza. What a wonderful end to a crisis of faith.

So that is where the book ends. I'm writing this now in my living room at home in the winter months. It's not been an easy three months, I've felt often bereft for leaving behind my old way of earning a living. I've had to trust that my family would be provided for and indeed we have even been, though it hasn't been easy. There have been many times that I nearly haven't written this book, but this final chapter, 'A crisis of faith' was the kick and encouragement I needed. So I close here by giving you two things; one a question – how does your ego work? What is ego to you? Rather than see it as an enemy why not try and work together through listening to your guidance?

Then finally as I prepared to close my laptop a Christmas message came through my channel, my gift to you;

'Today is 22nd December 2010, here is your Christmas message:

'Beloved keepers of the light, stay light within and without. Acknowledge your light within and as you acknowledge, feel it grow, feel it grow with love. Look at life and all of its splendour, show gratitude and see gratitude grow. Look at the children of today for they are the future of your tomorrow. Many of you are finding life hard at this time, I urge you to remember that you are loved even within your loneliness. Dig deep within and feel the love I have for you, feel it acknowledge its being and allow it to grow within you and without. You are not alone, I am right beside you urging you to continue, urging you to share in the journey of life, so if loneliness grips you at this time put your arms out to another. If you close your heart, your loneliness will prevail, so put your arms out and ask for help and it will come for you and to you. I am at peace and wish you peace, not only at this time but always. Jesus.'

I'm hoping that as you read these words you will feel the true beauty and the great love that resides within the meaning, so please keep your heart open, even in times of strife; it will be the greatest gift you give to yourself.

I hope this book has brought you peace. I send you love and gratitude for being part of my journey. Bless you. Thank you.

LESSONS LEARNT

- *Forgive others; they do not always know what they do.*

- *You always have the choice in how you react to any situation; you are your own creator. Do you choose to stay a victim or take ownership of your power?*

- *Learn to accept when a situation or friendship has come to its end.*

- *Learn to accept help.*

- *Look at how your ego works; work with it rather than against it. Challenge any thoughts of 'less than' or unworthiness.*

- *Observe your sabotaging behaviour and old thought patterns; are you ready to release them now? Acknowledgement brings healing to them, helping you to release them.*

- *Learn to nurture self, honour yourself as you would your best friend.*

- *Develop how YOUR guidance works and accept it.*

REFERENCE

Our Deepest Fear by Marianne Williamson, from *A Return to Love: Reflections on the Principles of A Course In Miracles*, Harper Perennial 1996

ABOUT THE AUTHOR

"Angel" Alison Ward is married with two sons and lives in the West Midlands. Her purpose and joy in life is to help others find themselves; their true angelic selves. Sharing her gift of intuition, guidance and channelling. Alison is available for one to one sessions and group EVOLVE channelling sessions either in person, by Skype or telephone. Please visit www.alison-ward.com to make your connection.

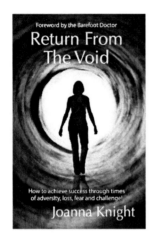

Return From The Void

How to achieve success through times
of adversity, loss, fear and challenge!

by Joanna Knight

Available from Amazon and
www.liveitpublishing.com

When You Think You Have Lost Everything... Think Again!

Based on her challenging and adverse personal experiences, combined with professional knowledge: Clinical Hypnotherapist and Stress Consultant Joanna Knight gives you her own unique insight, direction and philosophy into a tried and tested recipe for mental well-being, happiness and on-going success!

Learn how to:

Create room for mistakes to initiate growth	Notice fresh opportunities
Gain motivation, focus and clarity	Find out what you want
Release self-limiting patterns and beliefs	Discover your true potential
Discover your own truth with new awareness	Gain a powerful new perspective
Make your world work for you!	

"What I love about this book is that it takes into account that people are busy and want to get to the point quickly. Joanna does this, successfully blending candid, personal experience with simple yet extremely powerful methods to transform your life. Joanna's message is clear – if she can go from losing everything to gaining a life of happiness, health and success, so can you!"
Murielle Maupoint, Author of The Essential NLP Practitioner's Handbook.

"Joanna has taught me that through adversity you can rise from a 'Bottomless Pit' and come back 'Triumphantly'. Not only has she accomplished this, she has courageously written this for others to show them the way through!"
Liz Everett, Healer & Author of An Inner Light That Shines So Bright.

A-Z of the
Spiritual Life

God Death
Forgiveness
Romance Past lives Sex Crystal
Words Energy Channeling
Power Understanding
Love Future Soul Abundance
Meditation Astrology Awareness
Health Goddess Dreams
Nature
Questions

An Insider's Guide to the Spiritual Journey

Angela Courtney

A-Z of the
Spiritual Life

An insider's guide to
the spiritual journey

by Angela Courtney

Available from Amazon and
www.liveitpublishing.com

What might you experience
when living a spiritual life?

What secrets are there to discover?

If you need answers to the big
questions then this book can help.

Describing the author's experience of spirituality over the last 20
years it is packed with valuable advice, stories and observations
of a life created from the inside out.

Written in a lively but reassuring style the book is a series of
postcards on everything from Power to Past Lives, Sex to the
Sub Conscious. Including many unique descriptions of spiritual
experiences such as:

- How it feels to connect with your Higher Self
- How change is instant when you stop
  sacrificing what you want
- How Love comes to us when we meditate
- Understanding how relationships are our guide
  and what to do about it
- How we create everything in our lives including
  world events